I0008304

Mastering

# Baofeng Radios

The Complete Guide for Beginners & Experts to
Master Baofeng Radios

**Morgan Skye**

Copyright © 2024 **Morgan Skye**

**All Rights Reserved**

This book or parts thereof may not be reproduced in any form, stored in any retrieval system, or transmitted in any form by any means—electronic, mechanical, photocopy, recording, or otherwise—without prior written permission of the publisher, except as provided by United States of America copyright law and fair use.

**Disclaimer and Terms of Use**

The author and publisher of this book and the accompanying materials have used their best efforts in preparing this book. The author and publisher make no representation or warranties with respect to the accuracy, applicability, fitness, or completeness of the contents of this book. The information contained in this book is strictly for informational purposes. Therefore, if you wish to apply the ideas contained in this book, you are taking full responsibility for your actions.

*Printed in the United States of America*

# TABLE OF CONTENTS

# CHAPTER ONE

# A COMPREHENSIVE BAOFENG RADIO ANALYSIS

## An Overview of Baofeng Radio Analysis

Baofeng radios are becoming more and more common in amateur radio communication, piqueing the interest of both seasoned radio operators and newbies. These portable transceivers, made by Fujian Nan'an Baofeng Electronic Co., Ltd. in China, are a helpful starting place for two-way radio communication. Baofeng radios have proven useful in many situations, such as emergency preparedness and leisure activities.

## Baofeng Radios: The Evolution and History

The launch of Baofeng radios is a significant event that might be considered revolutionary in the fields of consumer electronics and amateur radio. It is important to first comprehend the origins and development of these technologies in order to gain a better grasp of how they have evolved into the everyday tools that they are today.

### Initial Steps

The early 2000s saw the establishment of China's Baofeng radio history at the Fujian Nan'an Baofeng Electronic Co., Ltd. in the province of Fujian. During this time, two-way radio communication underwent a significant change in the industry. This was due to technological advancements making reasonably priced, highly functional handheld transceivers possible. Baofeng Electronic Co., Ltd. acknowledged the growing need from businesses, consumers, and amateur radio enthusiasts for broadly accessible communication equipment. They not only had to fulfill this need, but they also had to come up with a solution that would challenge people's preconceptions regarding the device's performance, functionality, and cost.

### Novel strategies and incremental development

Since the start, innovation has been a major factor in the expansion of Baofeng radios. The business invested a large amount of money in R&D, using advancements in radio frequency engineering, semiconductor technology, and manufacturing techniques to improve its products on a constant basis. Originally, Baofeng's products were primarily designed to provide essential features at a reasonable cost.

Basic features like channel scanning, frequency tuning, and output power adjustment were frequently present in these radios. But as consumer preferences shifted and technology developed, Baofeng began to introduce more sophisticated models with enhanced functions. One important development that helped Baofeng radios gain traction was dual-band operation. For amateur radio operators and other radio enthusiasts, this feature created new options by enabling simultaneous communication on two different frequency bands.

## Growth and International Presence

As Baofeng radios became more well-known in China, the company decided to expand internationally. This was done in an effort to increase its appeal on a global scale. Baofeng profited from the global increase in demand for reasonably priced communication devices by leveraging the power of internet marketplaces and e-commerce platforms. Baofeng radios have become well-known throughout the world in part because they can operate on the most widely utilized radio frequencies and modulation types. This ensured that customers would not have significant technical challenges when incorporating Baofeng radios into their existing communication infrastructure across a range of countries. Baofeng's expansion objectives were largely successful due to their commitment to offering top-notch product support and customer service. To give customers access to replacement parts, warranty services, and technical support, the company established a global network of distributors and service centers.

## Constant Enhancement

The success of Baofeng radios can be attributed to its affordability and fair pricing, together with their dedication to continuous growth. With every new product generation, Baofeng sought to include innovative technology, listen to customer feedback, and broaden the scope of what was technically and functionally feasible. Even now, Baofeng radios are continually being produced, with each new model improving upon the successes of the last. In the amateur radio industry, Baofeng radios remain at the forefront of innovation, setting the bar for improvements in a variety of areas such as enhanced receiver sensitivity, extended battery life, and better digital signal processing capabilities.

## Distinctive Features and Abilities

❖ **Wide-ranging frequency range:** Baofeng radios often cover a number of bands, including VHF (Very High Frequency) and UHF (Ultra High Frequency), enabling users to communicate. Users can tune into numerous frequencies depending on their communication needs and the area they are working in thanks to this versatility.

- ❖ **The Dual-Band Operation:** Dual-band operation allows users to transmit and receive messages simultaneously on two different frequency bands. It is a feature found on a large number of Baofeng models. This functionality is especially useful for users who need to monitor many channels or interact with different bands, since it provides increased flexibility and convenience.

- ❖ **The Programmable Channels:** As standard equipment, Baofeng radios are built with the capacity to store and access programmable channels. Users can manually program channel frequencies, tones, and other options directly on the device. As an alternative, they can integrate more advanced programming capabilities by using computer software. By utilizing this feature, customers can adjust their radio settings to suit their unique communication requirements.

- ❖ **The Adaptable Output Power Settings:** Baofeng radios frequently have programmable output power settings, allowing users to control the radio's transmission power. Depending on the operational conditions and communication requirements, this capability can be very helpful in extending the transmission range or prolonging the battery's life.

- ❖ **The Backlit LCD Display:** Baofeng radios have an LCD screen that lights up at night to show vital data like the channel frequency, signal strength, battery level, and other relevant settings. It makes sure that users can quickly access important information by designing the display to be easily readable in a range of lighting conditions.

- ❖ **The FM Radio Receiver:** A built-in FM radio receiver is a feature of certain Baofeng radio models. This makes it possible for customers to continue listening to their favorite FM radio stations while they are not actively transmitting or receiving. This added capability, which also includes the ability to provide entertainment alternatives even when the radio is idle, extends the usefulness of Baofeng radios beyond two-way conversation.

- ❖ **The Voice-Activated Transmission (VOX):** Baofeng radios frequently include VOX pre-installed. This feature allows hands-free operation by turning on the microphone automatically when the user speaks. This feature is highly helpful because it allows the radio to be used independently in situations where manual push-to-talk operation would be uncomfortable or difficult, including when driving or performing other tasks.

- ❖ **The Monitoring and Scanning:** Baofeng radios frequently have features for monitoring and scanning that let users look for activity on a variety of frequencies or channels. This feature is useful for quickly detecting active frequencies during emergencies or events, or for monitoring multiple channels at once.

❖ Baofeng radios support the Continuous Tone-Coded Squelch System (CTCSS) and Digital Coded Squelch System (DCS) tones. Selective calling and receiving are made possible by these tones, which also help to reduce interference. These tones are compatible with Baofeng radios. Users can increase their capacity to communicate in noisy or crowded environments by filtering out unwanted signals with these tone-coded squelch devices.

❖ **The Compact and Portable Design:** Baofeng radios are renowned for their minuscule and lightweight designs, which make it simple to carry and use them in a range of indoor and outdoor environments. Whether hiking, camping, or engaged in emergency response tasks, their ergonomic form and lightweight build ensure that users remain comfortable even when using them for extended periods of time.

## Various Applications

❖ **Procedures of Amateur Radio (Ham Radio):** Baofeng radios are extensively utilized by amateur radio operators (hams) for a range of uses, such as taking part in local repeater networks, corresponding with other operators during competitions and events, experimenting with various communication modalities, and offering emergency communication support during public service announcements or disasters. They provide a multitude of additional functions as well.

❖ **External Recreation:** Baofeng radios are occasionally used by those who prefer to be outside for communication in remote locations where cellular service may be limited or nonexistent. Examples of these people include hikers, campers, hunters, and boaters. Using these radios enhances safety and convenience when going on outdoor excursions by facilitating group communication, coordinating efforts, and providing assistance in case of an emergency.

❖ **Disaster Reaction and Preparation:** Baofeng radios are essential tools for disaster response and preparation plans. Baofeng radios are used by volunteer organizations, search and rescue groups, disaster relief agencies, and community emergency response teams (CERT) to establish communication networks, coordinate rescue operations, disseminate vital information, and provides assistance during emergencies and natural disasters.

❖ **Public safety and security:** Baofeng radios are used for crowd control, internal communication, security patrols, and event coordination by small businesses, private organizations, security agencies, and event management firms. These radios allow people to communicate in real time, which facilitates quick responses to crises, emergencies, and security threats.

- ❖ **Production and Industrial Operations:** To promote coordination and communication between employees, managers, and supervisors, Baofeng radios are widely used in manufacturing plants, warehouses, and industrial settings. These radios help with workflow optimization, productivity enhancement, and safety improvement by facilitating prompt communication and cooperation between several departments and job sites.
- ❖ **Community & Neighborhood Watch:** To build communication networks to deter crime, perform surveillance, and report suspicious activity, homeowners' associations, community organizations, and neighborhood watch groups use Baofeng radios. These radios allow locals to stay in touch with one another, share information, and plan how to respond to emergencies and security threats in the community.
- ❖ **Fiestas and leisure pursuits:** Baofeng radios are employed by coordinators of festivals, events, and volunteer staff to enable efficient communication and coordination during open-air events, marathons, and other leisure pursuits. The successful management of the crowd and the smooth operation of the event are ensured by the use of these radios, which provide easy contact between the volunteers, security personnel, medical teams, and event staff.
- ❖ **Events related to Education and Training:** Baofeng radios are used in youth groups, training facilities, and educational institutions to impart radio communication skills, hold amateur radio license classes, and offer practical instruction in emergency communication protocols. The educational materials that these radios offer can be helpful to students, emergency responders, and anybody interested in becoming a radio enthusiast.

## Taking into Account and Limitations

Users should be aware of the constraints and limits associated with Baofeng radios before acquiring one or integrating them into their communication networks. Despite the fact that contemporary radios have many features, users still need to be aware of these issues and drawbacks.

This is a crucial list of things to think about:

- ❖ **Regulatory Compliance:** Government organizations, such as the Federal Communications Commission (FCC) in the US and equivalent bodies abroad, regulate the frequencies on which Baofeng radios operate. These authorities oversee Baofeng radios. It is the responsibility of users to make sure that their use of radio frequencies, acceptable transmission modes, and licensing requirements all comply with the relevant laws. Regulation noncompliance may incur monetary fines, legal ramifications, and disruption of licensed radio services.

❖ **Build quality and lifespan:** Despite the fact that Baofeng radios are well-known for their affordable costs, some customers have voiced worries about the radios' build quality and longevity, especially in hard or demanding environments. Users should assess Baofeng radios' construction and robustness in detail. A number of factors, such as shock resistance, water resistance, and overall durability, should be considered in this assessment to ensure that the radios can withstand the challenges related to their intended use.

❖ **User Interface Complexity:** Baofeng radios provide extremely complex user interfaces with a large range of settings, options, and features. For users who are unfamiliar with radio communication or who are just getting started, the complexity of the user interface may be frightening. There can be a learning curve for these folks to get the hang of the UI. To get the most out of the functionality and performance of Baofeng radios, users need be ready to invest some time in learning how to operate and configure the devices.

❖ **Programming and Software:** It might be challenging to program Baofeng radios with customized frequencies, channels, and settings, especially for individuals without prior technical experience. Though the keypad can be used to manually program Baofeng radios, most users choose to use computer software and programming cables for more effective programming and customization. For access to more advanced features and better radio performance, users must make sure their radio is compatible with firmware updates and third-party programming applications.

❖ **Restricted Customer Support:** Baofeng radios are frequently sold for less money than those made by more expensive radio manufacturers; however this usually entails less warranty coverage and customer support. There is a limited warranty on Baofeng radios. It may be difficult for users to get warranty services, troubleshooting guides, or technical support when buying Baofeng radios from unregistered dealers or online merchants. This is particularly true if internet retailers are used to buy the radios. Users should conduct due diligence on reputable manufacturers and suppliers who offer consistent after-sale support and customer help.

❖ **Compatibility of Accessories:** Baofeng radios might not be completely compatible with accessories made by other companies. Antennas, batteries, chargers, and earpieces are some examples of these accessories. It is imperative for users to confirm that their chosen radio is compatible with accessories made by reputable manufacturers in order to prevent any compatibility issues, performance limitations, or radio damage. Users should also be cautious when using low-quality or counterfeit attachments, since these items may compromise the radio's longevity and functionality.

## Selecting the Right Radio Model

Selecting the right Baofeng radio model is crucial, depending on your needs and tastes. Baofeng offers a large range of portable transceivers, each with unique features, capabilities, and price ranges.

The following factors must be taken into account when selecting a model for Baofeng Radio:

- ❖ **Frequency Range:** Very High Frequency (VHF) and Ultra High Frequency (UHF) bands are among the many frequencies that Baofeng radios often cover. However, because it can pass through barriers more easily than very high frequency (VHF), which is usually used for line-of-sight communication and works well in rural and outdoor areas, ultra-high frequency (UHF) is preferred for coverage in urban areas and indoor spaces. Think about the frequency bands that are often used in your area or by the people you want to connect with, in addition to your unique communication needs.
- ❖ **Power Output:** A radio's power output plays a crucial role in defining its signal strength and coverage area. Baofeng radios typically have power output options between one and eight watts, though they can be adjusted. Higher power outputs are generally associated with longer communication ranges and stronger signal penetration, especially in challenging environments or over obstacles. Having said that, higher power also consumes energy more quickly, so you should weigh your needs for longer battery life against your desire for higher range.
- ❖ **Channels & Programmability:** Baofeng radios have a few channels where you can store frequencies and configurations. This enables switching between different communication modes or frequencies easy. Think about the radio model's capacity to provide a lot of channels and how easily they can be programmed. While some models can be programmed with wires or additional software, others might have more user-friendly programming interfaces.
- ❖ **Battery Type and Life:** If you intend to use the radio for extended periods of time without having access to charging facilities, battery life is a crucial factor to take into account. Another crucial factor to take into account is the type of battery. Baofeng radios come with rechargeable battery packs, although some models also accept regular AA batteries or higher-capacity battery choices for

longer runtimes. It's crucial to consider both the many available charging options and your usual usage habits when estimating a device's battery life.

❖ **Dependability and Construction Quality:** A radio's dependability is crucial, especially if you want to use it outside or in harsh environments. When looking for Baofeng radio devices, you should search for models with a robust construction and features like shock and water resistance. Resilient enough to withstand weather exposure, mishaps, and rough handling, a sturdy radio can ensure reliable performance under the most trying conditions.

❖ **Extra Features:** Baofeng radios can include a lot of extra features on top of the basic communication features that make them available. Some of these features are the FM radio reception built-in, the LED flashlight, the emergency alarm capabilities, the dual-watch functionality (monitoring two frequencies at once), the VOX (Voice-Activated Transmission) feature, scanning modes, and others. After conducting an analysis, rank the features based on which are most important for your specific use case.

❖ Consider the Baofeng radio model's compatibility with various accessories, including headsets, antennas, microphones, and programming cords. While some models are compatible with standard accessories that are widely accessible in the market, others may include proprietary connectors or accessories. Furthermore, evaluate whether aftermarket accessories and amateur radio community support are accessible, as these can augment the adaptability and efficiency of your radio configuration.

❖ **Regulatory Compliance:** Verify that the Baofeng radio model you choose complies with all applicable laws and licensing requirements in your country or region before completing a purchase. It is imperative to select a radio that meets the regulatory requirements for authorized operation because amateur radio operators, in particular, are bound by certain license and frequency allotment legislation. Even though Baofeng radios are designed to abide by regulations in the majority of places, it is always a good idea to confirm specifications before making a purchase.

❖ **Budget:** You should set aside money for the purchase of your Baofeng radio, accounting for any further accessories or license fees that could be needed in addition to the radio's initial cost. Depending on the features, functions, and extras that come with the bundle, Baofeng radio prices can change. The affordability of Baofeng radios compared to other brands is well-known. Considering your financial constraints, prioritize the components based on the communication needs you have, and order them thus.

# Limitations on Radio Frequency (RF) Exposure

A set of guidelines known as radio frequency (RF) exposure restrictions is intended to protect people from electromagnetic fields, especially those produced by radios like Baofeng radios. These restrictions were put in place to protect people from possible health risks associated with extended exposure to radiofrequency (RF) radiation. Government organizations are in charge of establishing and implementing laws pertaining to radiofrequency radiation in the majority of countries. These organizations include the International Commission on Non-Ionizing Radiation Protection (ICNIRP), the Federal Communications Commission (FCC) in the United States, and others of a similar nature. There are laws governing radiofrequency radiation when it comes to radios and other emitters. To ensure the radio's electromagnetic energy stays within permitted bounds, certain guidelines must be adhered to when utilizing it in compliance with official regulations. One of the factors that the RF exposure limits take into account is the specific absorption rate (SAR), a method used to determine the rate at which the body absorbs radio frequency energy when it is subjected to interference from electromagnetic fields. One common unit of measurement for radiation that aids in defining the safe threshold is watts per kilogram (W/kg).

- **The frequency range:** Within the frequency domain, the human body can absorb and transmit various frequencies at varying depths and speeds. Different radiation levels for different frequency bands are typically specified by legislation.
- **Strength Levels:** The amount of radiofrequency radiation emitted by a radio emitter is determined by its power output. At lower power levels, there is typically less contact between the parts.

Like most commercial transceivers, Baofeng radios should abide by the national authorities' restrictions on radiofrequency exposure. Users are advised to follow the safety precautions provided by the manufacturer during the broadcasting procedure. One of the instructions is to keep your body at a certain distance from the radio antenna. It's important to remember, though, that despite worries about possible negative health effects from radiofrequency (RF) exposure, research in the scientific community has not yet shown a clear connection between emissions of radio frequencies below permissible levels and health hazards in humans.

Nonetheless, it's best to follow the safety instructions to prevent needless interaction. Following the manufacturer's instructions for antenna placement and use is essential to guaranteeing compliance and safety. Avoid the radio receiver at all times, especially when transmitting. Make sure you follow the laws and guidelines that establish the maximum level of radiofrequency radiation to which you may be exposed in your area.

## Different types of Baofeng radios

1. UV-5R Series
2. BF-F8HP
3. BF-888S Series
4. UV-82 Series
5. GT-3 Series
6. DMR Radios
7. Tri-Band Radios

## Regarding the UV-5R Series

Among Baofeng's several lines of portable transceivers, the UV-5R Series is one of the most well-liked and often utilized types. This series is quite popular among emergency responders, outdoor adventurers, and amateur radio enthusiasts because of its cost, ease of use, and versatility.

Among the notable characteristics of the UV-5R Series are:

- ❖ **Dual-Band Functionality:** The UV-5R radios can function on both the VHF (Very High Frequency) and UHF (Ultra High Frequency) bands thanks to their dual-band functionality. They can now access a wide variety of frequencies thanks to this. Furthermore, owing of this dual-band capabilities, users can communicate over a range of channels and frequencies, increasing their versatility and flexibility.

- ❖ **Compact and Lightweight Design:** These radios are incredibly portable and ideal for use in a range of situations due to their small and light design. Whether you're heading out on a trek in the woods, attending a public event, or engaging in emergency response-related activities, the UV-5R radios are portable and convenient to use while on the go.

- ❖ **Broad Frequency Coverage:** Users of the UV-5R radios can access a vast range of channels and frequencies for communication thanks to the radios' broad frequency coverage. Due to their broad coverage, these radios can be used for a variety of communication needs, from public safety frequencies to amateur radio bands.

- ❖ **Power Output Options:** Depending on the specific model under consideration, the UV-5R Series' power output options typically vary from 1 watt to 5 watts. To balance the signal strength and battery life, users can adjust the transmit power to suit their communication demands. Users can choose from this range of power output.

- ❖ **LCD Display and Keypad:** The radios have an easily navigable LCD display and an easy-to-use keypad that make it easy to program and adjust the radio's settings, channels, and frequencies. The user-friendly interface makes it easy for users to access and modify a wide range of features and guarantees hassle-free operation.

❖ **Built-in Features:** The UV-5R radios have a number of built-in features that enhance their usability and performance. These could include the emergency alert function, flashlight, voice-activated transmission (VOX), dual standby mode (which simultaneously monitors two frequencies), FM radio reception, and other functions.

❖ **Affordability:** The UV-5R Series' affordable price is one of its most noteworthy features. Baofeng radios are well known for offering outstanding value for the money, allowing users to take advantage of contemporary communication features without going over their budget. Due to their low cost, UV-5R radios are becoming a popular choice for both amateur radio enthusiasts and consumers who are worried about their budget.

## Regarding BF-F8HP

The high power output and enhanced performance features of the Baofeng BF-F8HP make it an exceptional portable transceiver. Compared to many other models, the BF-F8HP offers a stronger signal strength and a longer communication range because to its maximum power output of 8 watts.

Its dual-band working capacity allows users to send and receive on both the VHF and UHF bands. As a result, users now have greater alternatives and variety in their communication scenarios. This radio's improved antenna increases the efficiency of both signal transmission and reception. Improved coverage and clearer communication are assured, particularly in low-signal environments. Although the

BF-F8HP produces more power in its raw form, its effective power management capabilities allow it to maintain a reasonable battery life. Its power-saving modes and rechargeable lithium-ion battery pack ensure that it can offer consistent connectivity for extended periods of time.

The radio's robust design allows it to be used in harsh locations as well as outside. It offers dependability and durability for a variety of applications. Along with these advanced capabilities, the BF-F8HP also has an emergency alert function, dual standby mode, FM radio range reception, voice over internet protocol (VOX), configurable channels, channel scanning, and an emergency alert function. Outdoor explorers, emergency responders, preppers, and amateur radio enthusiasts have developed a devoted following for the BF-F8HP because of its outstanding performance, dependability, and affordability. Utilizing a compact and reasonably priced design, the BF-F8HP provides reliable communication performance for outdoor travel, emergency response situations, and ham radio operations.

## Concerning the BF-888S Series

The BF-888S Series is a range of single-band portable radios made by Baofeng. The main markets for these radios are the business and startup sectors. These radios are special because they are sturdy, affordable, and simple to operate. Ultra-high-frequency (UHF) frequencies are frequently used by them.

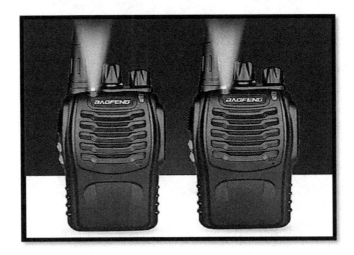

The BF-888S radios are a fantastic choice for a range of applications, including event management, retail, hospitality, security, and small-scale communication scenarios because they offer dependable communication in a compact, user-friendly form. They emphasize important characteristics and are well-built, which makes them perfect for settings where dependability and simplicity are crucial.

**Among the noteworthy characteristics of the BF-888S Series are the following:**

- ❖ **Single-Band Operation:** The ultra-high frequency (UHF) frequencies that are often found between 400 and 470 MHz are the only ones on which the BF-888S radios are intended to operate. This single-band operation ensures compatibility with UHF-based communication systems, which are commonly used in commercial and industrial contexts, and facilitates frequency management.
- ❖ **Compact and Lightweight Design:** These radios' small size and light weight make them portable and convenient to use in a range of situations. You can wear them on a belt clip or carry them in your pocket; either way, they offer a basic form of communication without taking up any additional space or weight.
- ❖ **Rugged design:** The BF-888S radios have a robust construction that can withstand drops, bumps, and other physical stresses that come with hard work environments. It is made to withstand the rigors of regular operation. Their strong building quality guarantees the long-term dependability and durability of their housing.
- ❖ **Basic Operation:** With simple controls and an uncomplicated user interface, the BF-888S radios are designed to offer a basic operation. Users may easily access essential features including channel selection, volume control, and push-to-talk (PTT) operation without requiring extensive technical knowledge or training.
- ❖ **Longer Battery Life:** These radios include rechargeable lithium-ion battery packs, which extends their battery life and lets them stay in constant connection for the duration of the working day. Because users can count on the BF-888S radios to keep working when they're most needed, there will be less disruptions and downtime. The radios' efficient power management features allow for this.
- ❖ **Basic Features:** With suitable accessories, the BF-888S radios may operate hands-free and feature voice activation (VOX), squelch control, channel scanning, and other essential communication features. They lack some of the more advanced capabilities found in dual-band or higher-end models, though.
- ❖ **Affordability:** One of the most important aspects of the BF-888S Series is its affordable price. These radios are made available to people, organizations, and businesses that are restricted by their financial resources because Baofeng is committed to offering communication solutions that are both economical and reliable—all without sacrificing their dependability or performance.

## The UV-82 Series

Baofeng produces a line of dual-band portable transceivers known as the UV-82 Series. Performance, reliability, and other state-of-the-art features are highly valued by the users of these transceivers. The UV-5R Series has been successful because of these radios, which offer a better experience with greater features and a more robust structure.

Similar to other Baofeng radios, the UV-82 Series has dual band functionality, allowing users to transmit and receive signals on both the Very High Frequency (VHF) and Ultra High Frequency (UHF) bands. Its dual-band capabilities enable communication across a larger spectrum of frequencies and channels, offering more flexibility and diversity. Compared to less expensive models like the UV-5R, the UV-82 radios are built with a stronger and longer-lasting construction. These radios' enhanced internal parts and ruggedized exteriors demonstrate that they are made to withstand harsh environments. The durable UV-82 radios can be used in outdoor activities, emergency situations, and industrial settings, among other situations. In order to enhance comfort and user experience, the ergonomic design of the UV-82 Series offers a larger form factor and better button placement. The radio's ergonomic design makes it comfortable to hold in one's hand, and its controls are easily accessible even in challenging situations or when wearing gloves.

A variety of state-of-the-art technologies are included with the UV-82 radios to enhance their functionality and effectiveness. Enhanced visibility and navigation with a larger LCD, extended battery life options, customizable channel names, twin Push-to-Talk (PTT) buttons for simultaneous conversation on two frequencies, and greater memory to store more channels and settings are just a few of these features. Users can access a wide range of channels and frequencies, including public safety and amateur radio bands, thanks to the UV-82 Series' extensive frequency coverage. Because of its extensive coverage, which ensures interoperability with a wide range of communication technologies, users can engage effectively in a number of scenarios. The UV-82 radios' channels are easily customizable, allowing users to save and recall their preferred frequency combinations with ease. Whether channels are being used for commercial applications, emergency situations, or amateur radio operations, the ability to set them up ensures effective and useful communication. Depending on the specific model in the UV-82 Series, additional capabilities could include FM radio reception, VOX (Voice-Activated Transmission), a flashlight, scanning modes, an emergency alert and other features. These features increase the radios' usability and adaptability, which qualifies them for a wider range of applications.

## The GT-3 Series

Baofeng is the manufacturer of portable transceivers sold under the GT-3 Series name. These transceivers are made for users who want their two-way radios to have more sophisticated features, longer battery life, and better functionality. Building on the popularity of previous Baofeng models, the GT-3 Series boasts a more robust design and increased functionality for an improved user experience. These radios now have improved performance features that lead to higher transmit power, more sensitive receivers, and overall improved signal quality. Practically speaking, this translates to improved audio quality, a greater communication range, and more dependable performance—even under trying circumstances.

The GT-3 radios' ruggedized design, which includes strengthened components and a robust exterior, enables them to withstand harsh use and outdoor conditions. Since these radios are made to withstand falls, bumps, and exposure to the elements, they can be used in a range of situations, such as emergency response situations, industrial settings, trekking, and camping. More advanced features have been added to the GT-3 Series, increasing its usefulness and usage. A larger LCD to enhance visibility and navigation, two Push-to-Talk (PTT) buttons to enable simultaneous use of two frequencies for conversation, extra space to store more channels and settings, and personalized channel names are a few potential features. Dual-band operation allows users to broadcast and receive signals on both the Very High Frequency (VHF) and Ultra High Frequency (UHF) bands on the GT-3 Series and other Baofeng radios. Its dual-band capabilities enable communication across a larger spectrum of frequencies and channels, offering more flexibility and diversity.

The radios have an ergonomic design that makes them comfortable to hold and an easy-to-use button layout. The radio's controls are arranged such that it is easy to reach the major functions, even in low light or when wearing gloves. The radio is made to be comfortable to hold in your palm. Users of the GT-3 Series can access a wide range of channels and frequencies, including public safety and amateur radio bands, thanks to the series' broad frequency coverage. Because of its extensive coverage, which ensures interoperability with a wide range of communication technologies, users can engage effectively in a number of scenarios. Users may easily save and remember their favorite frequency combinations with the help of the programmable channels on the GT-3 radios. Whether channels are being used for commercial applications, emergency situations, or amateur radio operations, the ability to set them up ensures effective and useful communication.

# Regarding DMR Transmissions

Handheld transceivers manufactured by Baofeng are called Digital Mobile Radio (DMR) radios. Those who favor digital communication methods are the target audience for these radios. When compared to digital mobile radio (DMR) technology, traditional analog radios offer greater privacy features, better signal quality, and greater spectrum efficiency. Moreover, audio generated with DMR technology has greater clarity.

Significant features of Baofeng DMR radios include the following:
- ❖ **Advanced Digital Communication:** Baofeng DMR radios send and receive data and speech signals using digital modulation techniques. Compared to analog radios, this digital communication technology has a number of advantages, such as less background noise, clearer speech, and more immunity to interference.
  Enhanced Security and Privacy: Encryption functions on DMR radios offer more security and privacy for private conversations. Users can make sure that their communications are private and safe from listening in on them or being intercepted by turning on encryption.
- ❖ **Text Messaging and Data Transmission:** DMR radios enable users to send and receive data packets as well as text messages in addition to voice communication. Sending brief messages, directives, or status updates to other radio users without vocal communication is made very convenient by this capability.
- ❖ **Superior Networking Features:** Baofeng DMR radios are equipped with sophisticated networking functionalities that enable them to establish connections with digital radio networks and systems. These networks provide smooth communication across huge geographic areas and can vary from local peer-to-peer connections to wide-area networks.

❖ **Dual-Mode Operation:** Certain Baofeng DMR radios have the capability to operate in both digital and analog modes, enabling users to choose the mode that best suits their communication requirements. This adaptability offers the advantages of digital communication technology while yet guaranteeing compatibility with current analog radio systems.

❖ **Broad Frequency Coverage:** Baofeng DMR radios often provide customers with extensive access to a variety of channels and frequencies for communication needs. Users are able to interact efficiently in a variety of contexts thanks to this comprehensive coverage, which also guarantees compatibility with different communication systems.

❖ **Simplicity of Use and Programming:** Baofeng DMR radios are made to be simple to use and operate, even with their sophisticated capabilities. The radios usually have simple programming options and user-friendly interfaces that make it easy for users to set up preferences, program channels, and access additional functions.

❖ **Compact and Portable Design:** Baofeng DMR radios are lightweight and compact, which makes them extremely portable and appropriate for use in a variety of settings. These radios are portable and easy to use while on the road, whether they are being utilized for professional purposes, outdoor activities, or emergency response scenarios.

## The Tri-Band radios

One kind of portable transceiver that Baofeng makes is called a tri-band radio. The purpose of these radios is to offer better frequency coverage than traditional dual-band radios. These radios have access to three different frequency bands. The VHF (Very High Frequency), UHF (Ultra High Frequency), and 220 MHz (1.25-meter) bands are often used.

**Baofeng Tri-Band radios provide the following vital features:**

❖ **Extended Frequency Coverage:** Customers can access three different frequency bands with tri-band radios, which provide extended frequency coverage compared to standard dual-band radios. More variety and flexibility are possible as a result of this improved coverage, allowing communication across a larger range of frequencies and channels.

❖ **Bands Covered by Baofeng Tri-Band Radios:** These radios usually operate in the VHF (136–174 MHz), UHF (400–520 MHz), and 220 MHz (220–260 MHz) frequencies. With distinct benefits and features offered by each band, users are able to select the frequency band that best suits their particular communication requirements and operational environment.

❖ **Better Performance:** Tri-Band radios can provide better performance in the form of stronger broadcast power, more sensitive receivers, and better signal quality all around. Practically speaking, this translates to a greater communication range, better audio quality, and more dependable performance—even under challenging circumstances.

❖ **Dual-Mode Operation:** Depending on the needs of the user for communication, users of some Baofeng Tri-Band radios can switch between analog and digital modes. This adaptability offers the advantages of digital communication technology when accessible, while simultaneously guaranteeing compatibility with current analog radio systems.

❖ **Sophisticated Features:** To improve functionality and usability, Tri-Band radios are outfitted with a number of sophisticated features. These could include two PTT (push-to-talk) buttons for transmitting simultaneously on two frequencies, a larger LCD for better vision and navigation, and increased memory to store additional channels and settings.

❖ **Ruggedized structure:** Tri-Band radios feature robust exterior and stronger internal components as part of their ruggedized structure. This design was created to withstand the harsh conditions and outdoor use. These radios may be used in a range of environments, such as industrial settings, emergency response settings, trekking, and camping, because they are made to withstand bumps, drops, and exposure to the elements.

❖ **Wide Frequency Coverage:** Tri-Band radios provide communication access to a multitude of channels and frequencies. Having wide frequency coverage over three bands allows for this. Because of its extensive coverage, which ensures interoperability with a wide range of communication technologies, users can engage effectively in a number of scenarios.

❖ **Programming and Usability:** Tri-Band radios are designed to be simple to use and operate, despite their many features. Additionally, programming is quite easy. The radios frequently have simple programming options and user-friendly interfaces that make it easy for users to set up channels, program channels, and access advanced features.

## DIY Exercises

1. Explain the Evolution and History of Baofeng Radios
2. What are the Distinctive Features and Abilities of Baofeng Radios?
3. What are the Various Applications of Baofeng Radios?
4. What are the constraints and limits associated with Baofeng Radios?
5. What are the factors that must be taken into account when selecting right model for Baofeng Radios?
6. What are the Different types of Baofeng Radios?

# CHAPTER TWO

# SETUP GUIDE FOR BAOFENG RADIOS

## Examining the accessories that are included

Numerous add-ons are available for Baofeng radios that can enhance the user experience overall.

Some of the items that might be very beneficial are as follows:

❖ Primarily, Wi-Fi antennae even though most Baofeng radios have a good-performing antenna that you may use on a daily basis; you might want to increase the radio's range. A more powerful receiver will enable you to accomplish this. The Baofeng Magnetic Antenna, Radtel Foldable Tactical Antenna, ABBREE AR-152A, and Nagoya NA-701C are a few of the most well-known Baofeng radio antenna variants.

## The management and configuration of Antennas

❖ Keep in mind that the device will have a Male SMA Connector, whereas the antenna will usually have a Female SMA Connector when aligning the connectors. Align these two connectors to make sure the antenna fits snugly, and then twist it clockwise until it locks in place firmly.
❖ To ensure correct antenna installation, spin the antenna into place while holding onto its base firmly. This technique guarantees both optimal performance and a secure attachment.

❖ It is imperative to keep an eye on the "SWR" (Standing Wave Ratio) while using an external antenna, aiming for a ratio of 1.5:1 or less. By keeping this ratio constant, possible harm to the receiver's transistors is reduced.

❖ Use caution when working with the antenna. Do not wrap it around things or hold it directly in your hand since these acts may cause it to perform poorly.

❖ Put functionality and safety first by making sure your smartphone is always connected to an antenna before sending out any messages. If the device is operated without an antenna installed, the apparatus may sustain harm.

## Concerning Belt Fasteners

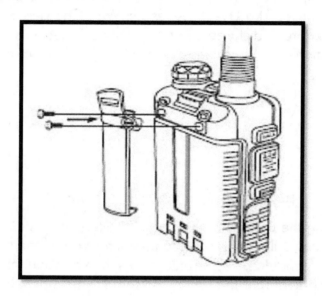

❖ Find the two screws that are next to each other on your radio's back, right above the battery compartment. Simply unscrew them in a counterclockwise motion to remove them.

❖ Line up the screws with the belt clip's matching holes. Make sure they are in the right place so they can easily pass through the perforations.

❖ Press the belt clip against the rear of the battery covers to secure it firmly, making that the holes in the clip line up exactly with the pins on the radio body. After aligning, put the screws back into the appropriate holes to secure the belt clip firmly.

❖ Don't use glue when attaching anything. The battery housing may sustain damage if adhesive is used. To guarantee a safe and secure attachment without running the risk of damaging the equipment, it is imperative to use the screws that come with the belt clip.

## About chargers or power converters

Users of Baofeng radios can fuel their devices in a variety of ways thanks to the radios' flexible charging options. Users usually use the charger that comes with the radio; this is usually a USB cord that plugs into a wall outlet or computer to provide power. When it comes to charging these radios from outside sources, such as solar power, USB connections, or 12V cigarette outlets, you do have some options. For those who want to charge many gadgets at once, buying a multi-unit charger may be helpful. The CH-5-6 Gang Charger, for example, can charge six nickel-metal hydride batteries, six lithium-ion single-cell batteries, or six lithium-ion dual-cell batteries simultaneously. The UV-5R Series Six Way Charger, on the other hand, expedites the procedure and shortens charging periods because it can charge up to six radios or batteries simultaneously—especially when managing numerous devices.

## Regarding the Battery Installation

The radio must always be turned off before handling the battery. Turning the power/volume knob all the way counterclockwise will accomplish this.

**The following are the steps involved in installing a battery:**

❖ **First, Orienting the Battery:** Make that the battery makes excellent contact and is positioned correctly with respect to the metal frame. The bottom of the radio and the battery should be separated by a space of about one to two inches.
❖ **Guided Attachment:** Set the battery so that it lines up with the radio frame's guide rails. To ensure a snug and safe installation, carefully slide the battery upward until it clicks into place.
❖ **Securing the Battery:** When the battery is placed, the radio's base battery latch clicks into action, securely securing the battery in place and preventing it from moving or coming loose while in operation.

## Regarding Battery Charging

To charge the battery, take the following actions:

❖ **Hook up the Power Adapter:** Start by attaching the charger base to the power adapter. Place one end of the adapter into the charging base's specified port.
❖ **Plug into Wall Outlet:** After that, insert the power adapter's opposite end into a wall outlet. In order to make the charger operational, this step gives it power.

- ❖ **Position Radio or Battery in charging location:** Place your radio or battery in the charger base's designated charging location. Make sure it is firmly and tightly fitting.
- ❖ **Check for Correct Alignment:** Making ensuring the battery's contact plates are properly positioned and in touch with the charger is vital. Verify that the radio is firmly positioned in the dock before charging. When the radio has a red LED light on, it is actively charging.
- ❖ **Track Charging Status:** See the charger's LED light while the radio charges. The LED light on the radio will turn green when it is completely charged. As soon as the radio gets full charge, take it out of the charger to avoid overcharging.

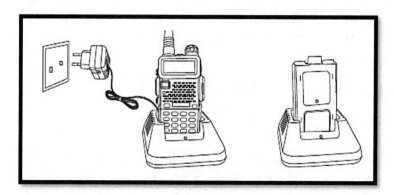

## Know the codes for the charger LEDs

| Charging Status | LED Indication |
|---|---|
| Standby (no load) | Red LED Flashes while Green LED glows |
| Charging | Red LED glows solidy |
| Fully Charged | Green LED glows solidly |
| Error | Red LED Flashes while Green LED glows |

## Remove the battery

- ❖ To remove the battery, make sure the radio is off. Make sure the radio is off before removing the battery. The electricity won't malfunction if you do this.

- ❖ Look for the battery's release. It should be placed on top of the battery pack. To remove the battery, press this.
- ❖ Press the button for battery release after swiping the battery down. Sliding the battery down a few centimeters will cause you to feel it separate from the radio's body.
- ❖ The radio can be totally removed by carefully taking it off and sliding the battery down a few centimeters.

## Turning it on and off

Using a Baofeng radio is simple. To get the screen to light up and the device to start beeping, simply push and hold the orange button located on the side of the kit. To turn off the radio, repeatedly press and hold the same orange button until a beep sounds and the screen turns black. This makes it easier to control the power and usability of the device.

# Crucial Functions and Rules

## Modifying the Squelch and Volume

- ✓ To turn on your Baofeng radio, crank the volume knob clockwise.
- ✓ Locate the radio's "Menu" button. To access the menu view, press it. The LCD screen will display the menu options.
- ✓ Navigate through the radio's menu selections by pressing the up and down button keys.
- ✓ Discover where the "Squelch" button is. Press the "Menu" button to pick it once you've located it.

1. Now that "Squelch" has been selected, you are able to adjust the squelch intensity. It is possible to adjust the squelch cutoff number by using the arrow keys. Lower numbers will cause the squelch to respond more strongly. This

implies that while the background noise may get stronger, weaker signals will still be able to be heard. The squelch loses responsiveness as the number increases. While it reduces background noise, weaker signals may be blocked out as well.

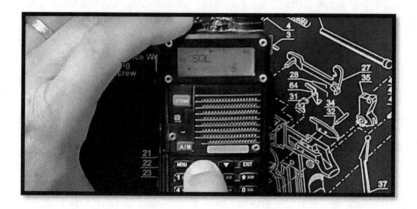

2. As you adjust the delay level, pay attention to the sound coming from the earphones or the radio's speaker. Reduce background noise as much as you can to ensure that you only receive the most critical signals.
3. Press the "Menu" button once again to save the changes if you're satisfied with the noise level. The menu mode on the radio will be removed.
4. Turn on the squelch by listening to radio noise. Ensure that the sounds you wish to hear are the only ones you can hear and that outside noise is not audible.

Keep in mind that the appropriate level of squelch may vary based on your activities and environment. It's best to experiment with a few settings until you determine which one best eliminates noise and signals.

## Selecting Frequencies and Channels

Baofeng radios are popular because they are affordable and widely adaptable. These radios can send and receive messages on a wide range of frequencies, making them useful for a number of scenarios, such as outdoor sports, emergency communication, and more.

**The following steps must be taken in order to identify channels and frequencies on a Baofeng radio:**

1. Press the VFO/MR button after turning on the radio in order to enter frequency mode.
2. You may use the up and down buttons to navigate and select the desired frequency.
3. Use the arrow keys and menu button to select T-CTCS or T-DCS. This will be the general tone.
4. Use the arrow keys to fine-tune and select the desired tone frequency.
5. To save the modifications, press the menu button once again.

Keep in mind that the Baofeng radio type you own may affect the frequency range and the channel selection procedure.

## A section of the radio's body and antenna

Baofeng radios are popular because they are affordable and widely adaptable. Because they are composed of sturdy but lightweight plastic, they are lightweight and portable. A small screen shows the station, battery life, and other settings. For communications to be sent and received, antennas are necessary. Although standard antennas typically function well, you can update the detector to extend the radio's range. Popular choices include the Baofeng Magnetic Antenna 1, Radtel Foldable Tactical Antenna, and Nagoya NA-701C. The purpose of these receivers is to facilitate the sending and receiving of radio messages.

## Batteries and Methods of Charging

There are various power options available to users of Baofeng radios. Using the charger that came with the radio is the main and most widely used way. These chargers typically come with a USB chord so you may use them with different laptops or power outlets. However, there are alternative methods for charging Baofeng radios, such as solar power, additional USB ports, or 12V cigarette lighter connections. Investing in a multi-unit charger will enable you to charge many gadgets faster. The CH-5-6 Gang Charger is an excellent choice since it can simultaneously charge six lithium-ion single-cell batteries, six lithium-ion dual-cell batteries, or six nickel-metal hydride six-cell batteries. Another excellent choice is the Six Way Charger from the UV-5R Series. It speeds up the process of charging numerous devices by simultaneously charging up to six radios or batteries.

# The buttons and screen

A Baofeng radio's body is typically composed of lightweight, portable plastic and is rather robust. Important information such as the station, power level, and other settings are displayed on the screen located on the radio's body.

## Understanding the Main Screen

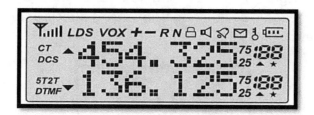

| Icon | Description |
|------|-------------|
| 188 | Memory Channel |
| 75/25 | Least Significant Modifiers |
| CT | CTCSS enabled |
| DCS | DCS enabled |
| + - | Frequency Offset Shift Direction if Enabled |
| S | Dual Watch/Dual Reception if Enabled |
| VOX | VOX Function if Enabled |
| R | Reverse Function if Enabled |

| | |
|------|-------------|
| N | Narrowband Enabled |
| ▭▭ | Battery Level Indicator |
| O⊔ | Keypad Lock Function if Enabled |
| L | Low Transmit Power Mode if Enabled |
| ▲ ▼ | Active Band or Channel |
| ▼ⅈⅈⅈ | Signal Strength Meter |

**You can explore the features and change the radio's settings by touching the following buttons:**

The VFO/MR button on your Baofeng radio is quite helpful since it makes switching between frequency mode and channel mode easy. The screen displays the whole list of all recorded frequencies in channel mode along with the unique call sign for each one, which in this case is "K5QHD." In addition to identifying registered repeaters, these call signs make them simple to find while in operation. You may more easily modify the radio by entering frequencies directly into the computer using the frequency mode.

A/B is another crucial button that facilitates switching between the top and bottom rows of channels. With a fast keystroke on the keyboard, you can switch between various channels.

The Band button comes in quite handy for switching between different frequency bands. You can move between the 70CM UHF band (420–450MHz) and the 2M VHF band (144–148MHz).

For listening to radio traffic and locating nearby repeaters, the Scan button is quite helpful. You can arrange the way you wish to view channels by holding down the look button. When you are first learning about the repeaters in your area, this is quite beneficial. Remember that although the sky may appear empty at times, hams often use networks from 7 to 8 p.m. on Monday through Wednesday. You should check your region frequently and at different times of the day to become familiar with it.

When you hit the "Call" button, a message is sent on the frequency you are now using. To avoid being interrupted, you should never hit this button while continuously scrolling through the channels.

To speak, you must push the PTT (Push-To-Talk) button. However, you need to obtain a ham license in order to use this feature. Never operate a radio without also connecting an antenna.

## A display of battery level

The battery is almost empty when there are no black bars visible. The radio will regularly beep and flash the display's backlight to let you know when to change the battery.

## The LED status

It shows three distinct operating modes:

- Green for receiving a signal,
- Red for transmitting, and
- Off for standby.

## The MONI button

- Turns off the mute to enable sound level assessment.
- Generates static noise, which is typically suppressed by the squelch function to aid in volume measurement.

## The Pound button

- Smoothly transitions between High and Low broadcast powers in channel mode.
- This is a one-time adjustment that won't impact settings in the future.

## The Lock on Keypad

- Blocks every button on the radio's side aside from three.
- Toggle the keypad lock by holding down the [POUND] button for approximately two seconds.
- You can activate automatic keypad locking from the menu.

## The Star-shaped button

- The ability to reverse is enabled with a quick press.
- When a live station is located, press momentarily to resume scanning while listening to broadcast FM.
- To begin continuous scanning, hold down the button for two seconds.

## DIY Exercises

1. Discuss the Numerous add-ons that are available for Baofeng radios
2. Explain the management and configuration of Antennas
3. What are the codes for the charger LEDs?
4. What are the steps that must be taken in order to identify channels and frequencies on a Baofeng Radio?

# CHAPTER THREE
# BAOFENG RADIO PROGRAMMING: MAXIMUM EFFICIENCY

## INTRODUCTION

Conversation takes place on a radio frequency, like 146.52. Many frequencies are used in radio communications. To avoid having to memorize them all, you can set them up like radio channels. Put another way, if you have 146.52 selected as your channel, all you have to do is keep in mind to tune in to channel 1 instead of the frequency. Alternatively, you can search through your list rather than entering each station individually. Simplex communication is the exchange of information between two devices using a single frequency. They would not be married if you were to have a conversation with someone listening in on frequency 146.52. Programming is the process of adding frequencies to channels. Repeaters are automatic devices that, after first listening for signal on a first frequency, "repeat" them on a different frequency. This becomes even more important when repeaters are utilized. Repeaters deal with greater problems. Many of them need a certain tone, called a CTCSS tone or a DCS tone, before they can play back the radio signal. The broadcast to that relay will not work if the correct tone is not programmed into the channel. Since repeaters utilize two frequencies, this type of communication is referred to as duplex rather than simplex.

## Programming on BaoFeng Simplex Channel

Since single frequencies are easier to manually set up than repeaters, this is a great place to start. You should begin in frequency mode rather than channel mode. When in frequency mode, you can directly set frequencies. When in channel mode, you can switch between previously chosen channels. Check the screen as soon as your BaoFeng is turned on. The channel numbers are displayed on the right side of the screen. As a result, you are currently in channel mode. Press VFO/MR to move between the two settings.

There are two sets of frequencies on the screen: one at the top and one at the bottom. The A/B button on the BaoFeng lets you quickly switch between two frequencies. To set a frequency, you must be on the top frequency, shown by a small line on the left.

When you are in frequency mode and on the top frequency, use the keyboard to input the desired frequency, such as 146.52. In line with this 146.520 The BaoFeng adds zeros to the end of an integer to enter a frequency. It is acceptable to input 146520 without a decimal point. Once the preferred frequency has been chosen at the top, press the Menu button. It is faster to input 27 rather than scroll to find the

MEM-CH menu option. The memory-based channel storage configuration is called MEM-CH. To change the MEM-CH setting, press Menu once you're there. MEM-CH will abruptly give way to CH-000, the regular channel, as indicated by the small line on the left.

**Hint:** Selecting "Exit" will always cause the settings panel to close. Both before and after the adjustments were saved, this functioned. You can input the name of the channel on the keyboard or go there with the arrow keys. Select the preferred channel, click Menu, and then click Exit to adjust the frequency. When you return to the main menu, press VFO/MR to enter channel mode. Use the arrow keys to get there or enter the code of the station into the keypad to confirm that it was configured correctly.

## Installing the BaoFeng repeater network

Once you know how to set up channels as simply as possible, repeaters can be added manually. The four main elements of repeaters that you should be aware of are the primary frequency, offset, offset direction, and tone. (RepeaterBook defines tone as "tone in" and "tone out"; for FM sources that work with the BaoFeng, these should match.) The repeater is broadcasting the primary frequency that you are now listening to. The offset shows the frequency on which the repeater is listening and on which you are sending. Offsets are represented by positive or negative numbers. Therefore, if the shift is -0.6 MHz and the rebroadcast frequency is 146.67 MHz, you send on 146.07 MHz. For this reason, you would broadcast on 147.27 if the difference was +0.6.

Utilizing W4CAT, a repeater in the Nashville area, as an example:

Frequency: 146.955
Offset: -0.6 MHz
CTCSS: 114.8

Repeat the previous few steps, being sure to enter the rebroadcast frequency and confirm that you are in VFO mode on the top frequency.
  ▪ **Define the offset direction**

> Press the Menu button.
> Press 25 or navigate to SFT-D.
> Press the Menu button.
> Use the arrow keys to toggle the offset direction (+/-).
> Press the Menu button to confirm.

- Adjust the Offset Frequency

> Press 26 or navigate to OFFSET in the menu.
> Press the Menu button.
> Enter the offset gap (-0.6 MHz, so type 000600).
> Press the Menu button to confirm.

- Select the CTCSS Tone

> Press 13 or navigate to T-CTCS (send CTCSS) in the menu.
> Press the Menu button.
> Enter the CTCSS tone frequency (114.8 Hz) using the keyboard.
> Press the Menu button to confirm.

Save the frequency to a channel using the same process as for simplex after all the settings are accurate. The offset direction, offset frequency, and CTCSS tone settings should all be saved to that channel. It's simple to confirm that everything was stored accurately. Find the channel that is rebroadcast. The plus sign (+-) should show up at the top of the screen to denote a shift. When you press the side PTT button to send, two indicators should show up: CT on the left, which indicates the sending of a CTCSS tone, and the frequency falling or increasing to the offset. In this case, the frequency moves to 146.355 for a -0.6 MHz shift and 146.955.

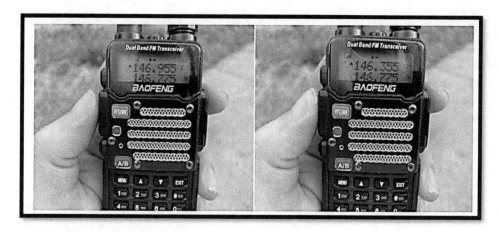

## How to get rid of a channel: A guide

It's much easier to eliminate a channel than to add one:

1. **Access the Menu:**
   - Press the Menu button on your radio.
2. **Select Delete Channel Option:**
   - Type 28 or scroll to DEL-CH using the arrow keys.
3. **Confirm Selection:**
   - Press the Menu button to confirm your selection.
4. **Choose Channel to Delete:**
   - Enter the channel number you want to delete using the numeric keypad or scroll to it using the arrow keys.
5. **Finalize Deletion:**
   - Press the Menu button again to execute the deletion process.

Proceed with caution as there isn't a confirmation prompt here. Press Exit before moving on to step 5 if, after accessing the menu, you decide to change your mind.

# Programming for Computers

This section assumes that your computer already has the Baofeng software installed.

## Connecting the Cable

Follow these procedures to connect the programming wire to your Baofeng radio and ensure proper configuration.

Take the following actions to make sure the control cord is compatible with your Baofeng radio:

1. **Turn off the Radio:**
   - Ensure your radio is turned off before connecting the programming cable. This precaution helps prevent any potential issues during the connection process.
2. **Locate the Accessory Port:**
   - Find the accessory port, typically located behind a rubber flap on the right side of the radio body. Open the flap to access the port.
3. **Connect the Cable:**
   - Insert the cable's ends into the appropriate ports on the radio. Ensure they are securely inserted and pushed down firmly to ensure a stable connection.
4. **Connect to Computer:**
   - Connect the USB plug of the cable to an available USB port on your computer.
   - Power on your computer and launch the programming software you'll be using.
5. **Turn on the Radio:**
   - After the cable is securely plugged in and the programming software is running, turn on the radio.

# About Baofeng software

- ✓ **Choose a language:** Baofeng's computer tools might initially launch in Chinese. Go to the second-to-right menu and select English from the list of language options to switch to English.
- ✓ **Channel Information Window:** This window frequently shows up when you run the programming software for Baofeng. If not, select Edit > Channel Information to view it.
- ✓ **Configuring Channels:** Set up the transmission port that the cable is connected to before adding any channels. Then, choose Program > Read from Radio, and click "Read" to bring any channel data from the radio into the application.

✓ **Connection Test:** By researching accessible channels, one can confirm that the programming line is connected appropriately. The radio's LED will become red if the read process proceeds as planned. This suggests that information is being transferred from the computer to the radio.

# Channel Information Window Definitions for Each Column

- ❖ **Channel** -> Channel number.
- ❖ **Band** -> Displays what Frequency Band is active.
- ❖ **RX Frequency** -> Receive Frequency.
- ❖ **TX Frequency** -> Transmit Frequency. Defaults to the Receive Frequency.
- ❖ **CTCSS/DCS Dec** -> Receiver CTCSS or DCS. Defaults to OFF.
- ❖ **CTCSS/DCS Enc** -> Transmitter CTCSS or DCS. Defaults to OFF.
- ❖ **TX Power** -> Transmit power. Defaults to HIGH.
- ❖ **W/N** -> Wideband or Narrowband operation. Defaults to W for Wideband.
- ❖ **PTT-ID** -> Enables and sets the position of PTT-ID. Defaults to OFF.
- ❖ **BusyLock** -> Busy Channel Lock-out. Defaults to OFF.
- ❖ **Scan_Add** -> Add to scanner list. When enabled the channel is included in scanning mode. Defaults to ON.
- ❖ **SigCode** -> Signal Code, group ID for the channel. Defaults to 1.
- ❖ **CH-Name** -> Channel name.

# Utilizing CHIRP Software to Program

These radios may be difficult to hand program. CHIRP software is a good way to solve the problem. We'll show you how to rapidly configure Baofeng radios with CHIRP so that you may be in constant communication with others.

## Blocking Frequencies on a Baofeng Radio with CHIRP

Have you ever thought about keeping your Baofeng radio set to the frequency you desire? With this, you'll have the security and privacy you need. These days, being able to choose the frequency your radio uses is essential. You believe that you are capable of sorting between conflicting cues to retain information and language that is understandable. Learn how to use CHIRP software and the world of Baofeng radio frequency blocking to take control of your radio experience by reading on.

## Understanding Baofeng and CHIRP Radios

CHIRP is one piece of software that boosts the power of Baofeng radios. Utilize this acronym to stand for "Comms Ham Radio Interoperability Programming." CHIRP is an open-source, cross-platform tool that is used to program several types of radios. Baofeng radios are among its main users. The wonderful thing about CHIRP is that it facilitates and improves radio communication. To make it easier to transfer programming data between your computer and Baofeng radio, CHIRP acts as a bridge. Users can change channels, frequencies, and other important parameters with complete control over the radio's settings. This degree of control is quite helpful, especially when weighing or halting in particular frequency ranges.

The intuitive interface of CHIRP, which was created with both inexperienced and seasoned radio users in mind, makes it stand out. Baofeng radios are easy to set up because of their simple design and limited number of menu options. To utilize CHIRP properly, you don't have to be a tech expert; it simplifies the process and saves you time and effort. Because it works with radios other than Baofeng, CHIRP is an excellent choice for people who own multiple brands of radios. This versatility expedites and streamlines the process by enabling you to apply your programming knowledge to different types of radios. Ultimately, Baofeng radios have gained popularity in the two-way conversation industry because they provide many users an inexpensive and adaptable choice. When used in conjunction with the CHIRP software, these radios become much more useful as programming and configuring them becomes effortless. Baofeng radios and CHIRP software make it easy and accurate to stay in touch, whether you're an amateur radio enthusiast or a businessperson who has to be able to communicate consistently.

## Why Frequency Blocking Is Important

To be able to jam out particular frequencies in the world of all the waves that surround us is like being able to play a key role in an intricate symphony using a range of instruments. It's not just a technological issue; it's also a sensible choice that may have an impact on a government agency that protects private information, a business that maintains confidential information, or a person who enjoys listening to radio. Let's talk about the significance of blocking certain frequencies and the potential consequences of leaving them unblocked.

# Reasons to Block in Order to Preserve Privacy and Security

- ✓ **Frequencies Maintaining Confidentiality:** The main goal of frequency blocking is to protect privacy. Anyone with the right equipment can pick up information transmitted over the radio. Frequency blocking makes sure your talks stay private and unseen by inquisitive eyes, whether you're talking about personal or private business matters. It's like hiding your windows from curious onlookers by drawing drapes over them when you're working inside.
- ✓ **Safety against spying:** In this day and age of high-tech gadgets and constant monitoring, eavesdropping is a worry for both people and businesses. By blocking particular frequencies, you can build a digital wall around your contacts to keep prying eyes from accessing private data. Your voice is protected like it is in a digital fortress.
- ✓ **Signal integrity:** If there are numerous radio systems in close proximity to one another, the signal integrity may be jeopardized. By keeping your communications apart from other broadcasts, frequency blocking aids in the maintenance of strong signals. Whether you are an amateur or an experienced responder, your radio signals need to be distinct and uncluttered.

# What Threats Are Associated with Open Frequencies?

- ✓ **Unauthorized Access:** Anyone who shouldn't be there can obtain access when frequencies are left unprotected. It's like having your front door open for anyone to come in without your consent. Discussions with unauthorized listeners may result in data leaks, privacy violations, and security vulnerabilities.
- ✓ **Data Vulnerability:** Data is critical in a world where connectivity is gaining ground. If your frequencies are available, then someone could change or steal your information. Without the appropriate frequency filtering, bad actors can access and change your data sources, damaging the operations and reputation of your company.
- ✓ **Disturbance and disturbance:** Frequencies that are left open may be impacted by unauthorized broadcasts or disruptions from other systems. This effect has the potential to misrepresent important messages, which could result in misunderstandings, slow reactions, and in some cases, even unfavorable outcomes.
- ✓ **Compromised Security:** Secure communications are essential for the military and security companies. Opening frequencies can put national security and public safety at risk by giving unauthorized people access to private channels.

These vital networks are protected from external threats via frequency blocking.

Lastly, the requirement to protect security, privacy, and communication integrity drives the strategic necessity of blocking particular frequencies. It's more than simply a gadget. Frequency blocking is the digital lock and key that protects your most valuable assets from prying eyes and possible attackers in a world where information is power. Due to the serious risks involved in keeping frequencies unprotected, blocking frequencies is not only a need in today's linked world, but also an option.

# Instructions on How to Start a Radio Broadcasting Career with CHIRP

In the dynamic realm of two-way radio communication, precision and adaptability are essential. Optimizing the performance of your Baofeng radio is similar to setting up CHIRP on your PC. Here's where the magic starts, where you may customize the frequencies, and where a delicate touch is the major draw. Let's go over how to get started with CHIRP, stressing once more how important having a suitable programming line is.

## All-inclusive Manual for CHIRP Configuration

**Installing and configuring:** To get the most recent software compatible with your computer, whether it is Windows, macOS, or Linux, visit the official CHIRP website (https://chirp.danplanet.com/projects/chirp/wiki/Home) and start your CHIRP adventure. After the download is finished, open CHIRP by following the prompts on the screen. Start this process with ease, even if you have no prior computer knowledge.

- ✓ **Connecting Your Radio:** It's important to connect your PC and Baofeng radio after configuring CHIRP. Using the correct programming cable is essential because it is what transmits data between devices. Connect the USB port on your computer to one end of the cord, and the programming interface on your Baofeng radio to the other. Make sure both devices are turned on and ready to communicate.

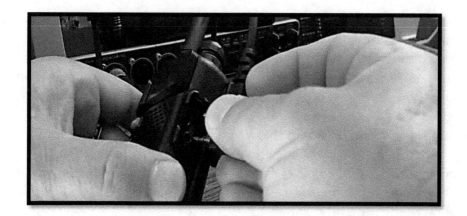

✓ **Radio Identification:** When you first launch CHIRP, it offers an easy-to-use, simple layout. The next step is to find out what kind of radio you have. Click Radio in the top bar, and then select "Download from Radio."

> ➢ From the "Radio" menu, choose the preferred brand, in this case "Baofeng." From the list provided, choose the model of Baofeng radio that you want. This is an important step since it guarantees that CHIRP satisfies the criteria of your radio.

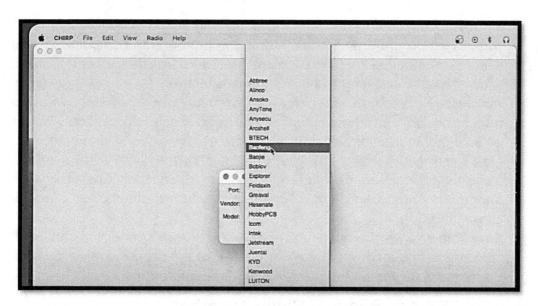

✓ **Read and Save Current Configuration:** Use CHIRP's "Read from Radio" option if you have already setup your Baofeng radio or would prefer to keep it that way. This utilizes the radio's settings and shows them on the software interface. Before making any changes, take care to backup this settings.

- ✓ **Choosing the Frequencies:** The procedure's most important step is this one. CHIRP's intuitive UI makes it easy to set up the necessary frequencies. Make new channels, enter their frequency ranges, and give them meaningful names. You can also change the broadcast power, delay, and tone settings. CHIRP's visual depiction of your channel lineup makes it simple to arrange and edit.
- ✓ **Putting something on Radio:** Now that you've carefully tuned your frequencies and channels, it's time to load this info into your Baofeng radio. After using CHIRP, all you have to do is click "Upload to Radio" and watch as your radio customizes itself to your tastes. After this step is finished, your Baofeng radio will be ready for use in conversation.

## The Value of an Appropriate Programming Cable

The programming wire is a crucial component in this intricate tango between radio modification and data transfer. This connection is required to link your radio to CHIRP on your PC; any other wire will not work.

**Here's why you require a device-compatible setting wire:**

- ✓ **Smooth Connection:** Your Baofeng radio and PC can connect seamlessly if you have a programming cable that is compatible with computers. It makes it less likely that there will be problems with data transfer or communication, which makes computing faster and more effective.
- ✓ **Accuracy & Precision:** Precision is essential when working with radio frequencies. As a proper connection is formed to send data reliably, you may be sure that the settings on your radio are exactly as you like them to be.
- ✓ **Data Integrity:** It's critical that your data be accurate. Data corruption during transmission can be avoided with a well-written code line. This is very important when using critical frequencies or channels for emergency communication.
- ✓ **Save time and effort:** Trying to survive with a broken connection can be time-consuming and inconvenient. With the use of the proper cable, you can set up more rapidly and simply, saving you time and effort.

### Linking CHIRP and Baofeng Radio Together

Setting up your Baofeng radio to function with the potent CHIRP software is the first step towards customized radio contact. You can customize the functionality of your radio to meet your needs by combining hardware and software when you delve into the realm of connections. To ensure a quick and easy connection, this section will walk you through the process of connecting your Baofeng radio to CHIRP. Additionally, it will discuss typical connectivity issues and offer solutions.

- ✓ Open CHIRP from the desktop. Press the "Radio" menu button, and choose "Download from Radio." Next, CHIRP will prompt you to pick "Baofeng" as the radio's manufacturer before letting you choose your preferred model from the list. By doing this, you can be confident that CHIRP is set up to work with your radio.

After that, CHIRP will make an effort to connect to your Baofeng radio and start a discussion. Verify that the COM port you have chosen in CHIRP's settings are the right one. If you are not sure which COM port to use, look for the port that is currently linked to your radio in the device manager on your computer.

- ✓ **As heard on the radio:** To proceed, click "OK" when the link has been generated. CHIRP will now read the current settings from your radio and display them on the software interface. This is an important step if you want to edit your current settings or save a copy of them.
- ✓ **Modify and Upload:** After seeing your radio's setup in CHIRP, you can make the necessary adjustments and modifications to the settings. You can change frequencies, add or remove channels, and tweak other settings as needed. When you're happy with your changes, click "Upload to Radio" to send the modified settings to your Baofeng radio.

## Frequently Asked Questions regarding Connection Troubleshooting

While it's usually not too difficult to set up your Baofeng radio to connect to CHIRP, mistakes do happen from time to time.

**Common connectivity problems are addressed by the following patches:**

1. **Select the Correct COM Port:** Confirm that the COM port you have chosen in CHIRP's settings is the right one. The radio and computer may not be able to communicate if the wrong COM port is selected.
2. **Verify Cable Integrity:** Ascertain the status of the programming cable. Communication may be hampered by broken or defective cables. Try using an alternative cable if you think the problem is with the current one.
3. **Install Drivers:** Verify that your computer has the drivers required for your programming cable installed. Driver software is frequently provided by manufacturers and must be installed in order for proper communication.
4. **Check Radio Compatibility:** Make sure CHIRP is compatible with the particular Baofeng radio model you own. If your radio model is not recognized by the program, compatibility problems may occur.
5. **Verify Radio Power:** Switch on your Baofeng radio and connect it to the computer at the same time. In order to establish communication, power is needed for both the radio and CHIRP.
6. **Experiment with Different USB Ports:** Attach the programming cable to an alternate USB port on your PC. Communication problems with particular USB ports might occasionally occur.

# Configuration of the backup radio

## Radio Configuration Backup: Preserving the Digital Legacy of Your Radio

When you communicate over the radio, you carefully choose each frequency, channel, and configuration to meet your specific needs. Similar to this, your radio's digital fabric or setup draws attention to its unique features. Your professional skills, inclinations, and communication needs are all blended into this digital DNA. This gem should never be in danger of disappearing. This is the point at which backing up your radio's setup with CHIRP becomes essential; in this section, we'll explain why this is the case and walk you through the process appropriately.

## The Advantages of Setting up a Backup

✓ **Preserving Individuality:** The setting of your Baofeng radio is a flexible tool that matches your preferred method of use. Whether you've carefully set up frequencies for emergency calls or channels for entertaining, this personalization shows that you know what you need. You can keep your precious digital board from losing any unexpected data by making a backup.

- ✓ **Protection Layer against Data Loss:** In the unpredictable realm of technology, there are many reasons why data loss might happen, software bugs and unforeseen events being just two. Knowing that you can use a backup copy of your radio's settings to bring it back to optimal performance in the unlikely case of data loss gives you peace of mind and acts as a kind of safety net.
- ✓ **Replication Efficiency:** Owning many Baofeng radios or sharing your setup with others is easier when you have a backup. You can quickly copy settings between devices so you don't have to start from beginning. By doing this, time is saved and consistency is guaranteed.

## Utilizing CHIRP to Store Your Present Configuration

- ✓ **Press CHIRP to begin:** To begin, make sure your Baofeng radio is plugged in with the correct programming wire and open the CHIRP application on your PC.
- ✓ **Read aloud on the radio:** Click "Radio" in the menu when CHIRP opens, and then click "Download from Radio." By doing this, CHIRP will be able to connect to your Baofeng radio and retrieve its current settings. You want to keep this configuration's security intact.
- ✓ **Preserving Configuration:** When your radio's settings appear on the CHIRP screen, choose "Save As" from the "File" option. Select a suitable name for the backup file and save it in a spot on your computer. Make sure the file type ".img" is chosen so that it can be recovered at a later time.
- ✓ **Last Actions:** Once the location and name of the backup file have been determined, click "Save" to create it. These files contain all of the stations, frequencies, and radio settings that CHIRP will use.
- ✓ **Validation:** By visiting the location where the backup file was kept, you can confirm that it is present on your computer. You should routinely check the security of your saved files to make sure they remain valid.

## DIY Exercises

1. Explain the Installation process of the Baofeng repeater network
2. What are the Reasons for Blocking in Order to Preserve Privacy and Security?
3. What Threats Are Associated with Open Frequencies?
4. Address Common connectivity problems in setting up your Baofeng radio to connect to CHIRP
5. Explain how to utilize CHIRP to Store Your Present Configuration
6. Discuss the Advantages of Setting up a Backup

# CHAPTER FOUR
# AN INTRODUCTORY RADIO COMMUNICATION COURSE IN A FLASH

## Handling Basic Radio Protocols for Two-Way Communication

Pushing a few buttons and talking is insufficient to get over the barriers of two-way radio communication. It's crucial to comprehend the unwritten rules and etiquette that underpin conversations in order to conduct polite, fruitful, and open ones. Imagine yourself dancing, where balance and rhythm are maintained with each stride. Let's be clear first things first. Put yourself in this situation: you are running a busy operation where it is critical that everything be clear. It's in situations like this that having clear and concise communication skills becomes crucial. Slang and non-essential terminology should be avoided as they can lead to additional confusion. Alternatively, aim for precise and succinct communication. Think of your words as beams of light that cut through the shadows and guide your team toward success. Alright, let's talk about introductions now. It's polite to introduce yourself at a gathering before striking up a discussion. When you press the PTT button, you will have the chance to say something like, "Hey folks, this is [Your Name/Call Sign] checking in." Everyone around you can see that you are conversing with this slight motion, which encourages more natural conversations.

But before you continue, wait a minute for the talk to wind down. It's like waiting for the cue to come in a play. Is there a conversation going on right now on the channel, or is there nothing at all? In addition to being polite, waiting one's time also helps avoid awkward situations where someone inadvertently interrupts someone else. When you do speak, it's critical to keep in mind that the words you use should forward the discourse. "Out" denotes a courteous pause in the discussion, "Over" indicates that you've completed speaking and are waiting for a response, and "Roger" acknowledges. These sentences set the tone and ensure that everyone is speaking at the same time as they serve as the discussion's center. Similarly, make sure that every letter you write is clear and concise. Since things move swiftly in radio communication, conciseness is your best friend. Compared to writing a novel, you might compare it more like texting someone. Make your opinion clear, make your position known, and then offer people an opportunity to respond. A disagreement is never resolved if you don't pay careful attention. Consider yourself a part of a jazz group in which players alternately play solos. When it's your turn to sing, pay attention to the chords other people are playing and don't start picking up notes. By doing this, you're not only showing consideration for other communicators but also keeping things from getting out of control. Now let's talk about the mood. Just like you wouldn't want to cut off a heated discussion at the coffee shop, background noise can negatively interfere with radio transmissions. To avoid distractions, switch off your radio while you're not using it and locate a quiet area. Keep in mind that any beeping, rustling, or buzzing could be an interference causing the information to cease flowing. You should consider this. Privacy is also another crucial component.

Remember not to reveal critical information over open channels, just as you wouldn't shout out your personal information in a public setting. Always act professionally, and reserve the heated rumors for private conversations. Lastly, it's imperative that you understand the rules of the game. Every organization and jurisdiction has its own set of regulations and procedures that apply to radio transmission. Learn about these guidelines and make sure you follow them to the letter. Envision yourself mastering intricate dance moves, where every step has a distinct function and placement. Conducting a symphony is like learning the basic manners of a two-way radio conversation. It is the duty of every member to contribute in unison, paying attention to the cues and the timing. If you can master these etiquette, you'll not only ensure that communication is seamless but also cultivate a polite and professional culture within your team. Therefore, remember that politeness, clarity, and communication are essential for success the next time you turn on the radio.

## Speaking the Language: A Clear Analysis of Radio Jargon

- ❖ **10-codes:** These obscure codes enable rapid and effective communication between radio users, much like a covert handshake. What do they mean, though? Alright, let's examine a couple instances. Most renowned is undoubtedly "10-4", which stands for "Acknowledged" or "Message received." Saying "Got it, loud and clear!" is akin to that. Next is "10-20," which translates to "Location" or "Where are you?" It's a convenient method to find out someone's location without having to give a detailed explanation.
- ❖ **Over and Out:** Ah, the traditional sign-off on the radio. However, what distinguishes "Over" from "Out"? Consider "Over" as a way to interrupt a conversation to let the other person know you've finished speaking and are waiting for a response. As if to say, "Your turn!" Conversely, "Out" signifies the last farewell and the conclusion of the discussion. Saying "I'm done talking; see you later!" is how it sounds.

- ❖ **Roger That:** This is an old favorite. What does that mean, though? Said another way, it means "Message received" or "Acknowledged." It's similar to giving someone the thumbs up to indicate that you clearly understood what they were trying to say.
- ❖ **Copy That:** This expression functions similarly to "Roger that," meaning "Message received" or "Acknowledged." Saying "Got it, no problem!" is akin to that.
- ❖ **Affirmative or Negative:** Rather of merely responding with "Yes" or "No," radio operators frequently employ these phrases to confirm or refute a claim or request. That's like to stating, "Yes, that is accurate," or "Nope, that is incorrect."
- ❖ **Standby:** Before answering, there are instances when you need time to collect your thoughts or double-check anything. In this situation, "Standby" is useful. It's equivalent to saying, "Wait a minute; I'll be right back."
- ❖ **Mayday:** This is a serious one. It's the standard distress cry in an emergency that signals the need for quick aid. Saying "Help, I'm in trouble!" is how it feels.
- ❖ **Break, Break:** Let's say you are having a chat when all of a sudden there is an urgent matter to discuss. At such point, priority traffic should be interrupted and conveyed using "Break, Break". "Hold that thought; I need to jump in with something important!" is how it would sound.
- ❖ **ETA (Estimated Time of Arrival):** Organizing logistics or setting up a meeting? Your best friend is ETA. It serves as a signal for the anticipated time of arrival at a given place. It functions similarly to saying, "I'll be there around [insert time here]."
- ❖ You've undoubtedly heard the terms **"Alpha, Bravo, Charlie, etc."** used to form letters on the radio. However, why not just read the letter aloud? Well, utilizing such a phonetic alphabet helps prevent confusion, particularly in tough or noisy circumstances. It's similar to having a precise and unambiguous secret code.
- ❖ **Squawk:** This is a term that many in the aviation industry have undoubtedly heard before. It alludes to a transponder code that is used on radar to identify airplanes. It resembles an electronic signature floating in midair!

Now you are the owner of all information! This simplified version of the radio jargon will help you relax. Whether you are an experienced radio operator or a beginner just starting out, knowing this terminology can help you communicate clearly and confidently on the air. Lift up your mic, pay attention, and let's get this conversation started!

# Learning to Utilize the DCS and CTCSS Tone Appropriately

The Continuously Coded Squelch System (CTCSS) and Digital-Coded Squelch (DCS) are two two-way radio communication systems that protect privacy and reduce the likelihood of an accidental interruption. These characteristics are popular among amateur radio operators, which is why Baofeng radios are often seen with them. Learning the DCS and CTCSS tones can greatly improve the efficacy of conversations.

## An Overview of CTCSS and DCS

- ✓ **CTCSS or Continuous Tone-Coded Squelch System:** To send and receive messages, CTCSS uses an inaudible tone. The radio only transmits when it detects a signal with the correct CTCSS tone. Each user or group of users is allocated a unique tone.
- ✓ Digital-Coded Squelch (DCS): This more modern method substitutes digital codes for analog tones. Just like CTCSS and the radio won't break the quiet until they receive the correct digital code, every person or group has a code.

## How to set up Baofeng radios for DCS and CTCSS

- ✓ Press the MENU button on the radio to view the menu.
- ✓ To get to the "CTCSS" or "DCS" setting, use the arrow keys.

- ✓ Decide whether DCS code or CTCSS tone is suitable for the channel or group you want to talk to.
- ✓ Save the changes to make sure they take effect.

## Selecting Suitable Codes and Tone

✓ Work together as a group: To facilitate communication, be sure that everyone in your contact group is using the same DCS tone or CTCSS code.

✓ Study the frequency tables. Frequency charts with the matching DCS code and CTCSS tone are available in several places.

## Why using CTCSS and DCS is a good idea

✓ **Less disruption:** CTCSS and DCS lessen the chance that other users on the same channel will disturb other users by removing signals that have the wrong tone or code.

✓ **Privacy:** You can establish a private channel of communication on a shared frequency by using different tones or codes.

## Common Errors and Ideal Methods

✓ **Compatibility:** Ensure that users are able to handle CTCSS and/or DCS and that they can set the proper codes and tones on each radio in your group.

✓ Before depending on CTCSS or DCS in an emergency, make sure your radios are properly equipped and able to communicate with one another.

## An emergency communication

✓ Disabling DCS or CTCSS may be necessary in an emergency in order to speak with those who aren't carrying these devices.

## Legal Aspects

✓ Learn about the DCS and CTCSS tone laws in your area to make sure you are following the law.

# Strategies for Group Interaction

# Establishing and Organizing Radio Groups

## Channel Programming

❖ Getting to the Menu To access the menu options, press the Menu button on your Baofeng UV-5R radio.

- ❖ **Finding the Memory Option:** To find the Memory option in the menu, use the up and down arrow keys. Once it's highlighted, choose it by pressing the Menu key.
- ❖ **Choosing a Memory Channel:** Go through the options and select the memory channel that you want to keep. To confirm your choice, press the Menu button once the channel of your choice has been highlighted.
- ❖ **Entering Frequency:** To enter the frequency for the chosen channel, use the keyboard. To verify and save the frequency to the memory channel after inputting it, click the Menu button.
- ❖ **Repeat for Additional Channels:** To add a channel to your groups, follow the steps mentioned above. To do this, navigate to the Memory option, choose the memory channel you want, input the frequency, and then press the Menu button to confirm your entry.

## The Channel Task for Groups

Arrange channels into groups according to the tasks at hand.

For example:

> **Group 1:** Emergency channels
> **Group 2:** Channels related to work
> **Group 3:** Personal communication channels

The software channels each one at a time into specific memory places or numbers based on the groups you've selected.

## Labeling and identifying groups

- Give these groupings names or labels to make them simpler to find on the screen.
- From the Memory choices, choose the channel you want to name, and then use the keys to type the name in.

## Configuration for Dual Watch/Dual Standby (Optional)

- Utilize the dual standby and dual watch features of the Baofeng UV-5R radios to watch multiple shows simultaneously.

- Set these settings to control how different frequencies or groups interact with one another.

## Priority setting and channel scanning

- Use the monitoring tool to keep an eye on or pay greater attention to specific group channels.
- Make use of the monitoring and prioritizing tools to keep an eye on the most important channels for each group.

## Testing and Making Adjustments

- Verify that the features are functional by switching between channels and groups to make sure they are appropriately labeled and ordered.

## Specific Phone Conversations

A channel of communication may become overloaded with messages when a lot of people use it to communicate. There are ways to get rid of unnecessary or too many SMS so you can manage them all. Individual or group calling is possible with a two-way radio. Group calling enables you to speak with several people at once. Since every radio is configured the same way, you can talk to anyone in the group and everyone will be able to hear you. Individual callers utilize pagers, which work similarly to a private chat. Only by providing a code that corresponds with theirs can you communicate with a specific radio. It's like using a cell phone to make a call.

Three options are available for group calls on the Baofeng UV-82 radio:

```
1. CTCSS
2. DCS
3. Tone-burst (1750Hz)
```

However, as of right now, the Baofeng UV-82 lacks a personal calling capability. It's crucial to keep in mind that other users can still hear your texts when using group chat. These technologies just aid in the removal of unnecessary material. People without equivalent filters can still hear your calls, no matter what voice settings you choose.

# Putting Together Announcements and Group Calls

## Speak with a User Group

❖ **Select the Channel:** To select the channel that corresponds to the talk group name or ID, use the channel button.

❖ **Handle and Place the Device:** Hold the walkie-talkie up and away from your mouth by about 1 to 2 inches (2.5 to 5 cm).

❖ **Press the PTT Key:** To start a call, press the Push-To-Talk (PTT) key. The discussion group alias or ID and the group call sign appear on the screen when the LED light turns red.

❖ **Release to Listen:** To listen, let go of the PTT key. When the other radio responds, the LED light becomes green. The screen displays the other walkie-talkie's ID or alias as well as the call group details.

❖ **Channel Idle Tone:** If this feature is activated, when the other radio has finished transmitting, you will hear a short beep. This means that you have the channel to yourself to respond. To respond, use the PTT key. After a predetermined amount of inactivity, the call ends.

❖ **Returning to Normal Screen:** The walkie-talkie screen goes back to what it was before the call finished. Your address book can be used for additional purposes, such as group calls.

## Concerning CTCSS

This technique allows you to designate a distinct tone frequency that functions as a "key" for filtering out undesired communications from the channel.

Use these instructions to configure CTCSS on your Baofeng radio:

❖ **Getting to the Menu:** To access the menu settings, press the [MENU] button.

❖ **Choose Receiver CTCSS (R-CTCS):** To view the Receiver CTCSS settings, enter [1] [1] on the numeric keypad.

❖ **Verify Selection:** To verify your choice, click the [MENU] button.

❖ **Enter Receiver CTCSS Frequency:** Enter the appropriate CTCSS sub-tone frequency in hertz using the numeric keypad.

❖ **Save Settings:** To confirm and save the CTCSS frequency you have selected, press the [MENU] button.

❖ **Choose Transmitter CTCSS (T-CTCS):** To access the Transmitter CTCSS options, press [1] [3] on the numeric keypad.

❖ **Verify Selection:** To verify your choice, click the [MENU] button.

- ❖ **Enter Transmitter CTCSS Frequency:** Enter the appropriate CTCSS sub-tone frequency in hertz using the numeric keypad.
- ❖ **Save Settings:** To confirm and save the CTCSS frequency you have selected, press the [MENU] button.
- ❖ **Leaving the Menu:** To leave the menu settings after finishing the configuration, click the [EXIT] button.

**To deactivate CTCSS and go back to regularly utilizing channels:**

- ❖ Proceed as per the previous instructions, with the exception that in step 4 and 8, insert [0] in lieu of a sub-tone frequency.
- ❖ To ensure that you want to save your choices, click the [MENU] button.
- ❖ To close the menu, press the [EXIT] button.

The CTCSS Table, which is part of the Technical Specifications section near the end of your radio's handbook, has a comprehensive list of all conceivable CTCSS codes and the accompanying sub-tone frequencies.

## Getting rid of a channel or frequency

- ❖ Hit the MENU button.
- ❖ Go with option 27/28.

- ❖ Press the MENU key to change channels.
- ❖ Decide the frequency or channel you want to stop listening to.
- ❖ To get rid of it, hit MENU once again.
- ❖ Go out.

# Look for frequencies and transmitters that are operational

It's possible that you're in a disaster-affected area and aren't sure which frequencies or channels to use.

In this case, you can still hear emergency calls by using the UV-5R to scan the airways:

- ❖ **Switch to Frequency Mode:** Press the VFO/MR button to make sure the radio is in frequency mode.
- ❖ Turn on scanning by holding down the "SCAN" key until scanning starts.
- ❖ **Scan Interrupt:** The radio will briefly halt scanning to listen in the event that it identifies a broadcast.
- ❖ **Modify Scan Frequency Jump:** To access scanning settings, press the MENU button.
- ❖ **Choose "STEP":** To choose "STEP," navigate to the menu and hit MENU.
- ❖ **Select Step Size:** To choose the appropriate step size for frequency scanning, use the up and down arrow keys.
- ❖ **Recognizing Step Size:** Both scanning depth and speed are impacted by step size. Slower but more thorough scanning is possible with smaller step sizes (e.g., 2.5K). While scanning is faster with larger step sizes (e.g., 50K), frequencies may not be covered as comprehensively.

## Switch the operating band of the radio (UHF or VHF)

Baofeng uses two frequency bands: Very High Frequency and Ultra High Frequency. Only one of the two bands may be used and viewed at once.

**To change the band:**

- ❖ **Access the Menu:** To access the menu settings, press the MENU key.
- ❖ Select "BAND" (Option 33). Navigate the menu selections until you reach option 33, denoted as "BAND."
- ❖ **Choose "BAND" Option:** Press the MENU key once more to bring up the "BAND" option.
- ❖ **Select VHF or UHF:** Toggle between the VHF and UHF bands according to your preferences by using the up and down arrow keys.
- ❖ **Verify Selection:** Press the MENU key one again to verify your selection.
- ❖ **Exit Menu:** After making your decision, close the menu.

Remember those emergency medical services, law enforcement, the government, and rescue operations use the VHF band for emergency radio frequencies.

# DCS and CTCSS "PL" or "private line" communications

On rare occasions, a large number of operators will send and receive signals on the same radio frequency. This will probably happen in a dire circumstance. To maintain constant contact, a lot of command centers, emergency response teams, and rescue operations will employ a single frequency. However, tonal frequencies are used to maintain a specific distance between each operator that shares a frequency in order to prevent transmission overlaps and congested airways. The terms Continuous Tone Coded Squelch System (CTCSS) and Digital Code Squelch (DCS) relate to these tone frequency systems.

**The digital nature of DCS is the primary distinction between the two systems.**
- ❖ The 50 universal tones in CTCSS are expressed in hertz (Hz).
- ❖ The 105 universal tones (DO23N) that DCS provides are numbered A through Z.

Think about the cellular network that runs a wireless phone to have a better understanding of this. The frequency itself is like the network, and the CTCSS or DCS tone is like the phone number. You must be connected to the network in order to send and receive data, and you must "dial" the correct number—either the CTCSS or DCS—in order to converse. The UV-5R's tone settings are already set up to function with both systems. When sending, you need to be aware of the tone that the suitable frequency is utilizing.

## How to Use a Channel or Frequency to Program CTCSS and DCS

**To program a CTCSS or DCS tone into a frequency that requires it, save it on a channel:**

- ❖ **Enter Channel Mode:** To enter Channel Mode on the radio, press the VFO/MR button.
- ❖ **Choose Channel A:** If needed, use the A/B button to confirm that you are on Channel A.
- ❖ **Enter Frequency:** Type in the frequency you want to save using the numeric keypad.
- ❖ To view the menu, click the MENU icon.
- ❖ **Configure Transmitting and Receiving DCS Tones:** To configure the transmitting and receiving DCS tones, respectively, navigate to choices 10 and 12.

- ❖ **Establish Transmitting and Receiving CTCSS Tones:** In a similar manner, select choices 11 and 13 to establish the relevant CTCSS tones for transmitting and receiving.
- ❖ **Verify Settings:** To ensure that you have selected each tone, press the MENU button one more.
- ❖ **Modify Tones:** In choices 10 and 12, or 11 and 13, choose the appropriate DCS or CTCSS transmitting and receiving tones using the up and down arrow keys.
- ❖ **Verify Selection:** To verify your choice for every tone, press MENU.
- ❖ **Preserve Frequency and Tones:** To preserve a channel's frequency as well as the transmit and receive DCS or CTCSS tones, select option 27.
- ❖ Exit: Click this to close the menu settings after finishing the programming.

The frequency you just stored should now be visible on the screen, with "DCS" or "CT" to the left of it.

## Methods for Recognizing Radio Frequencies

### What makes VHF and UHF frequencies different?

The choice between a VHF and UHF model is one of the most important factors to take into account while searching for two-way radios. Depending on the size of the organization, the location of the team, and the budget, each person requires a different amount of time. Having said that, what matters and what does your company need? The main difference between these two solutions is the frequency spectrum they use. But it doesn't stop there.

## What makes VHF and UHF frequencies different?

### Very high frequency radio (VHF)

VHF radios operate in the wider broadcast zone of the 30 MHz to 300 MHz radio wave spectrum. Compared to traditional two-way radios, they have fewer channels, which may cause crowding and crosstalk. VHF radios are often more affordable and have a longer history than UHF radios. Extremely high frequency two-way radios are perfect for long range and outdoor applications. This is because their signals get weaker in places where there are a lot of obstacles, such high-rise buildings. Additionally, they work best in settings with few people so they may do activities without being interrupted. VHF radios work better in leisure and agricultural environments overall.

## Ultra-high frequency, or UHF, radio

UHF two-way radio waves are less mobile than VHF radio waves because of their shorter range. But because they cover a larger frequency range, they do offer better service with less interference from other customers. UHF radios require more frequent battery changes due to their higher operating frequency. Therefore, employees shouldn't utilize charging outlets if they are difficult to get. The fact that UHF radios can transmit through materials like steel, concrete, and wood makes them ideal for use in urban areas. For this reason, interior applications such as manufacturing, distribution, healthcare, and education are where this type of radio works best, even in multi-story buildings. Businesses who operate in areas with a high concentration of nearby buildings and both indoor and outdoor space may also find them useful.

## To sum up

Variable-frequency radios (VHF) are perfect for usage in broad areas and unimpeded outdoor settings due to their extended range. Because of their higher frequency, UHF radios are perfect for wireless communications that have to go through concrete, walls, and other obstacles. Because of this, UHF radios work best indoors, where there may be walls and other obstacles.

## Guidelines and Frequency Ranges

Certain Baofeng radio models, including the BF-F8HP, GT-3TP, and UV-5R series, operate in politically restricted frequency ranges. The Very High Frequency (VHF) and Ultra High Frequency (UHF) bands are where these radios are most frequently used. But remember that you have to abide by local laws and license requirements, and that the frequencies that these radios can utilize can differ depending on the nation.

**These frequency ranges are covered by most Baofeng radios:**

- ❖ VHF (Very High Frequency):
  - ✓ **Frequency Range:** 136 MHz to 174 MHz.
  - ✓ **Usage:** VHF is used for a number of things, such as FM broadcasts, amateur radio (ham radio) operations, maritime communication, and public safety communications.
- ❖ Ultra High Frequency (UHF):
  - ✓ 400 MHz to 520 MHz is the frequency range.

✓ Applications for UHF frequencies include amateur radio operations, public safety radio systems, business radio communication, and other specialized communication services.

Baofeng radios usually have access to a large range of frequencies within these bands. This enables communication between users over multiple channels that are designated for different purposes. However, it's crucial to remember that not all frequencies in these regions can be correctly accessed without the required authorization. The laws controlling the use of these radios vary on a national and regional level. It is frequently forbidden to transmit communications on frequencies designated for emergency services or the government without the required permit or license. For instance, radio transmission in the US is governed by the Federal Transmission Commission (FCC). The appropriate FCC license is required in order to use a Baofeng radio and transmit on amateur (ham) radio frequencies. Users also have to abide by the restrictions on other services or frequencies to avoid legal issues. To ensure they are using the frequency bands appropriately and lawfully, users should be aware of local regulations and license requirements before using Baofeng radios. If you wish to support law-abiding radio broadcast and promote responsible radio transmission, you must obtain the necessary permits or authorization.

## DIY Exercises

1. Discuss the Clear Analysis of Radio Jargon languages
2. Explain How to Use a Channel or Frequency to Program CTCSS and DCS
3. What makes VHF and UHF frequencies different?
4. Discuss the Guidelines and Frequency Ranges

# CHAPTER FIVE

# AN UNDERSTANDING OF THE ANTENNAS

## Antenna Types and Applications

Baofeng radios are generally referred to as handheld transceivers, or just HTs. These radios come with an assortment of antennas that are suitable for various uses.

Some common types of antennas and how they function with Baofeng radios are as follows:

- ❖ **Rubber Duck Antennas:** These are the standard antennas that come with Baofeng radios. They are suitable for activities like hiking, camping, and event organizing when there is a restricted area for short-range communication because of their mobility and simplicity of use.
- ❖ **Whip Antennas:** Compared to rubber duck antennas, whip antennas are longer and perform better. They can boost the range and clarity of your radio's signal, making them ideal for outdoor activities when you need a bit extra range, including hunting, outdoor sports, or search and rescue missions.
- ❖ **High-Gain Antennas:** These antennas are designed to increase signal strength and increase the effective range of your radio. They can be utilized for long-distance communication or in areas with poor signal coverage, such as remote locales or crowded metropolitan areas.
- ❖ **Directional Antennas:** These include panel and yagi antennas, which direct radio waves in a certain direction to allow for more concentrated communication over longer distances. They are commonly used in point-to-point communication arrangements or for linking to distant repeater stations.
- ❖ **Dual-Band Antennas:** Baofeng radios are usually dual-band and can operate on both VHF and UHF frequencies. Since dual-band antennas are designed to perform effectively in both frequency bands, communication is more flexible with them.
- ❖ **Base station antennas:** These can be fixed or semi-permanently arranged. Since these antennas are larger and more powerful than portable ones, they frequently provide higher signal strength and a longer range. They are commonly used for amateur radio setups or the establishment of communication hubs in emergency situations.

When choosing an antenna for your Baofeng radio, consider factors such as the intended use, the operating environment, and the desired range. Verify compatibility with both your radio model and the desired frequency bands.

## Overall compatibility with FRS, MURS, GMRS, and Ham radios

❖ **Ham Radio (Amateur Radio):** Like many other portable transceivers, Baofeng radios are widely used in the amateur radio community. They span a large range of frequencies, including those used only for amateur radio. These radios frequently include multi-band and multi-mode capabilities and may transmit and receive signals on a range of amateur radio bands, such as 2 meters (144-148 MHz) and 70 centimeters (420-450 MHz). Their affordability and versatility make them a popular choice among amateur radio operators, particularly for testing, disaster relief, and mobile operations.

❖ **General Mobile Radio Service (GMRS):** Although the FCC has not officially authorized its use, Baofeng radios can be set up to transmit and receive on GMRS frequencies (462-467 MHz). However, it's crucial to keep in mind that GMRS cannot legally operate without an FCC license. Some users still use Baofeng radios on GMRS frequencies, despite the FCC's prohibition on using radios not authorized for GMRS usage. Users must ensure that they are in compliance with all licensing requirements and are aware of any FCC restrictions before using Baofeng radios on GMRS frequencies.

❖ **FRS (Family Radio Service):** Designed for short-range communication between family members and small groups, the FRS frequencies (462-467 MHz) are license-free. It is also possible to set up Baofeng radios to function on these frequencies. But if Baofeng radios are used on FRS frequencies, there may be legal ramifications, just as with GMRS. For radios to be considered compliant with the FCC's rules on the devices that can be utilized on FRS channels, they have to meet a number of requirements. Baofeng radios may work on FRS frequencies, but in order to avoid fines, users must make sure they abide by FCC regulations.

❖ **MURS (Multi-Use Radio Service):** License-free MURS (Multi-usage Radio Service) frequencies (151–154 MHz) are available for use by Baofeng radios for both personal and business purposes. The five communication channels in MURS have a longer range than those in FRS. Baofeng radios are suitable for a variety of applications, including outdoor activities, small businesses, and community groups, since they can be set up to transmit and receive on MURS frequencies.

## Differentiating Between GMRS and FRS Radio Signals

Users of personal radio services frequently inquire about the distinctions between FRS (Family Radio Service) and GMRS (General Mobile Radio Service) devices. Even if they are similar, it is important to recognize their differences. First off, the 462-467MHz frequency region in the UHF band—which includes 22 well-known simplex channels and frequencies—is where both FRS and GMRS radio function. Consistent channel assignment allows radios from different brands and models to easily converse with one another. The licensing required is the main distinction, though. Since FRS radios don't require a license to operate, they are legal to buy and use. However, you must pay for a license in order to operate a GMRS radio. User communication for both services is improved by the ease with which FRS and GMRS radios may converse with one another in spite of having different licenses. When the FCC tightened the regulations controlling GMRS and FRS in 2017, sales of combination radios that supported both services were discontinued. Customers began to inquire about the distinctions between the two services, despite the fact that the goal of these modifications was to remove any possibility of confusion. Furthermore, even though GMRS and FRS radios operate in the same way, there may be differences in each model's power output, range, and other features.

When choosing a radio for use at home or at business, these functional distinctions need to be taken into account. Fundamental differences exist between FRS and GMRS radios, despite their shared features and frequency ranges, unique functionality, and separate licensing requirements. Understanding these distinctions can assist you in adhering to regulations and determining whether using radio necessitates a GMRS license. There are only portable handheld models of Radio

Category FRS radios available. Additionally, only channels 8–14 can be used by GMRS devices for base stations and mobile stations; broadcasting is not permitted on these channels. Because of this, a number of GMRS radio manufacturers don't even think to incorporate these channels into their basic and portable models. Energy Level an FRS radio can only have a maximum power of 2 watts on channels 15–22 and 1–7, whereas a GMRS radio can have a maximum power of 50 watts on channels 15–22 and 5 watts on channels 1–7. Although power differential is typically the first consideration when talking about radio performance and range, it's not always as significant as one might think, particularly in the case of portable handheld devices.

# About the Removable Antenna

The distinctions between General Mobile Radio Service (GMRS) and Family Radio Service (FRS) with regard to radio legislation include things like how each radio is built and operated, particularly with regard to antenna standards. FRS radios require their antennae to be secured in situ; removing them would damage the equipment irreparably. Attempting to remove such an antenna is not advised as you will be in violation of both the law and the warranty on the radio. In addition, it lacks aesthetic appeal. On the other hand, GMRS radios can be mounted on vehicles, structures, or towers as long as their exterior antennas remain below a certain height limit.

They are also permitted to have detachable antennae. Although fixed antennas are typically used to identify FRS radios, it's crucial to remember that this isn't always the case. Furthermore, it's likely that some older GMRS portable radios with antennae permanently affixed were produced prior to the 2017 Part 95 Reform. However, a radio that possesses one of these characteristics is automatically categorized as GMRS because Family Radio Service prohibits the use of detachable antennae. The need that they have an immovable antenna further explains why FRS mobile or base station radios are nonexistent. The use of a remote antenna attached to a feed line, which is usually necessary for these devices, is prohibited by FRS regulations. Because of this, the primary function of FRS radios is their ability to function as portable devices with antennas that are permanently attached.

## Repetitive Ability

Although the 22 channel and frequency designations for both systems are the same, the GMRS has access to 8 more repeater channels, for a total of 30 channels. FRS does not have access to these repeater channels and is not allowed to transmit on repeater systems.

# Approved by the FCC

For a radio to fall within the FRS (Family Radio Service) or GMRS (General Mobile Radio Service) categories, it must be of the Part 95 type and hold an FCC certification. This classification is indicated by the FCC ID on the radio. If a radio has received type clearance for Part 95B, it is considered FRS. On the other hand, it falls under the GMRS radio category if it has Part 95E certification. Find the FCC ID on the radio and compare it to the FCC website to find out a model's service classification. The FCC's decision is final and authoritative in this instance. It's important to keep in mind that neither radio station is permitted by law to use radios without an FCC ID. A radio must be FCC type certified for that particular service and have a current FCC ID associated with the model in order to be utilized with any of the personal radio services provided by the US. Compliance with regulations is essential, even if enforcement falls outside our purview. The service classification and whether a license is required to operate the radio can be ascertained using the previously described differences between GMRS and FRS radios. Which service type is ideal for a particular radio depends on each of these factors.

# Antenna Gain and Polarization: An Understanding

The amount that a signal is focussed or amplified during transmission is measured by its antenna gain. As a result, the signals get stronger and wider. An thorough understanding of antenna gain can make it much easier for amateur radio operators to establish reliable long-distance connections. Consider the following hypothetical situation: A radio operator in a distant mountainous area hundreds of kilometers away would like to get in touch with other amateur radio operators. Circuits must always be visible and operational, even in situations where resources are scarce and the terrain is challenging. This is where antenna gain comes into play, providing possible fixes for problems like poor signals brought on by geographical or environmental obstacles.

## How to Recognize Loss in Antenna

Let's assume for the purposes of this paragraph that you are getting ready for an extended phone conversation. Antenna gain is still the most important component that will determine whether or not your broadcast is successful, even after you have assembled and calibrated your equipment to the correct frequency. We'll talk about antenna gain in this part and stress how important it is to get the strongest signal possible. An antenna's capacity to focus sent or received signals in a particular direction is known as antenna gain. It measures the power that an antenna emits in a specific direction as opposed to an ideal isotropic radiator, which generates the same amount of power in all directions. To help you understand this better, let's look at a real-world example study: Assume that two antennas placed next to each other have the same transmission strength. How could you tell the difference between the two if their rates of increase were different? The power and range of the signal would increase with a higher gain antenna by concentrating more energy in the desired direction.

**The following advantages must be taken into account in order to understand why antenna gain is so important:**

❖ **Enhanced Signal Strength:** Higher gain antennas can magnify signals from weaker sources, improving communication and facilitating connection establishment.

❖ **Extended Range:** Antennas with higher gain can reach farther than those with lesser gain. Their coverage area is improved as a result of their increased directional focus, which enables longer signal transmission.

❖ **Lessened Interference:** By limiting their transmission pattern, high-gain antennas reduce interference from neighboring sources and undesired noise. Even in congested or noisy areas, this targeted transmission aids in maintaining signal clarity.

❖ **Improved Reception Quality:** Talks and communications have crisper sound quality with less distortion and interference when a stronger signal is received via high-gain antennas. Experiences with communication become more efficient and seamless as a result.

**The following table lists the several popular antenna types along with the appropriate gains:**

| Type | Gain (dBi) | Applications |
|------|-----------|--------------|
| Yagi-Uda | 10 | Long-range point-to-point links |
| Dipole | 2 | General-purpose, short-range usage |
| Parabolic | 30 | Satellite communication |
| Log-Periodic | 8 | Wideband communications |

Since antenna gain directly impacts the efficiency of their communication system, understanding it is crucial. By selecting the appropriate antenna with the appropriate gain, operators may achieve the most signal strength and range with the least amount of clutter.

# Classifications of Antenna Gain

It is imperative that people who want to become more proficient communicators understand Antenna Gain! In the last part, we discussed the concept of antenna gain and how it might enhance signal transmission and reception. **Let's now discuss the various types of antenna gain that are frequently employed in more depth.**

- ❖ **Directivity:** Increasing the directivity of an antenna improves its gain. The signal gets stronger where it is focused and less elsewhere when the energy pattern is directed in that particular direction. For example, when speaking over long distances or in difficult terrain, such communicating from a mountain to a station at sea level, utilizing a highly directional antenna with high directivity gain can considerably increase transmission clarity.
- ❖ **Efficiency:** The ability of an antenna to convert input power into electromagnetic waves is referred to as its efficiency. Stronger signals can go farther using antennas with higher efficiency. The antenna with higher efficiency—typically attained through improved design or superior materials—will transmit a stronger signal even if the two antennas have the same gain in decibels (dB).
- ❖ **Beamwidth:** The angle at which an antenna can transmit or receive signals without suffering a noticeable reduction in performance is known as its beamwidth. Greater directivity and better gain in the covered area are implied by a narrower beamwidth. On the other hand, a larger beamwidth may result in less gain per unit area covered by sacrificing some directivity in favor of greater coverage.
- ❖ **Front-to-Back Ratio:** This indicator shows how successfully an antenna separates signals coming from behind it from those coming from the desired direction. An antenna that successfully rejects signals from undesirable directions will have a high front-to-back ratio, which will increase gain and signal clarity. This capacity is especially important in areas where there is a lot of noise or interference.
    - ✓ Enhanced directivity facilitates targeted transmission and reception
    - ✓ Longer range and stronger signals are the results of higher efficiency.

- ✓ Higher gain is possible within a smaller coverage zone with narrower beamwidth.
- ✓ Higher front-to-back ratio guarantees enhanced differentiation between intended and unwanted signals.

## About Markdown Table

| Type | Explanation |
| --- | --- |
| Directivity | Focusing the radiation pattern towards a specific direction |
| Efficiency | The ability of an antenna to convert input power into radiated electromagnetic waves |
| Beamwidth | The angle over which an antenna can effectively transmit or receive signals without significant loss in performance |
| Front-to-Back Ratio | Measures the ability of an antenna to discriminate between signals received from the desired direction versus those coming from behind it |

In conclusion, individuals who enjoy listening to the radio and wish to improve their speaking abilities ought to be aware of the many kinds of antenna gain. Operators can select antennas based on factors including front-to-back ratio, beamwidth, efficiency, and directivity to get stronger signals, longer range, and better overall performance. After examining the topic's many components, let's examine the factors that influence antenna gain in more detail to develop a deeper understanding of the topic.

## Factors Governing Antenna Gain

Now let's go into more detail about the various kinds of antenna gain that you need to be aware of. One important kind is called directional gain, and it describes the ability of an antenna to focus radiation in a specific direction. For long-distance transmission, this could lead to notable fluctuations in the signal's power and quality. Imagine that you are trying to get in touch with a fellow Ham who lives on a far-off island. You can boost the likelihood of a successful transmission by directing the energy you send in that direction by using an antenna with a high directed gain. Reflector gain is another type. This type adds more parts or structures, which raises the signal intensity and total radiation pattern. These mirrors lessen radiation in other locations by emitting energy in a focused manner. It works in a similar way as when you place mirrors strategically around your antennas to boost signal strength when it matters most. Parasitic element gain, often known as "the power of companionship," is another element gain technique that takes advantage of the cooperative behavior of several antennas. This is accomplished by putting extra parts—also referred to as directors or mirrors—in close proximity to the primary driving source. These additional components, which are calibrated and positioned properly, can help concentrate and direct the emitted energy more successfully than it could be with a single antenna.

To sum up:

- ❖ **Directive Gain:** Directs energy in a certain direction to maximize contact across long distances.
- ❖ **Reflector Gain:** By including extra parts or structures, this type of gain enhances radiation patterns.
- ❖ **Parametric Element Gain:** This improves performance by facilitating communication between adjacent antennas.

Knowing the different types of antenna gain can help amateur radio operators choose the appropriate gear for their needs. Next, we'll talk about measuring antenna gain, which is an important step in figuring out which antennas work best.

### Estimation of Antenna Gain

One of the key factors influencing an antenna's gain is its size. Larger antennas typically offer better gains because they can gather more electrical energy from their surroundings. It's also critical to remember that expanding an antenna might not always be feasible. Another crucial element is the antenna's design. The percentage of gains varies throughout groups. A Yagi-Uda antenna, for instance, can be utilized for long-distance transmission since it usually offers good gain and directivity for point-to-point communication. Dipole antennas, on the other hand, have the ability to transmit signals in any direction, although their gain may be less than that of directed antennas. An antenna's operating frequency has a significant impact on its gain as well. Antenna efficiency varies with frequency range, and they are often designed to operate within certain frequency ranges. It is essential that you choose an antenna that is suitable with the frequencies you plan to use if you want to maximize its gain potential. Let's now invent a tale about two radio enthusiasts named John and Sarah. They decided to install HF (high-frequency) antennas for their respective locations.

**The following table presents a comparison of the key factors affecting antenna gain:**

| Factor | John's Antenna | Sarah's Antenna |
|---|---|---|
| Physical Size | Large | Small |
| Design | Dipole | Yagi-Uda |
| Operating Frequency | 3-30 MHz | 14-30 MHz |
| Expected Gain Potential | Moderate | High |

In this case, Sarah selects a smaller Yagi-Uda antenna with a higher gain potential at the frequencies she wishes to use, while John selects a larger dipole antenna with a wider frequency range. You can select the ideal antenna for your requirements if you are aware of the factors influencing antenna gain. To maximize the performance of your wifi connections, choosing the appropriate antenna gain is crucial. Now let's discuss some key points to consider and some advice to assist you makes an informed decision.

## How to Choose the Best Antenna Gain

Imagine that you are eager to test out your new antenna after finishing the construction of your amateur radio station. Measuring the gain of an antenna is one approach to evaluate its quality. This section discusses the different methods that radio enthusiasts can use to determine antenna gain precisely.

So let's begin by examining a few widely used methods for figuring the antenna gain:

- ✓ **Measurement of Field Strength:** A standardized field strength meter can be used to determine the signal strength at different distances from the antenna. The gain of the measured antenna can be ascertained by contrasting these values with those obtained from a reference antenna.
- ✓ The single-antenna method uses a single antenna in conjunction with a reference source that has a known power output and radiation pattern. The precise gain of the tested antenna can be calculated by measuring the received power in different directions around it.
- ✓ **Two-Antenna Comparison:** By carefully limiting characteristics like direction and distance and using one antenna as a test and the other as a reference, direct comparisons between two antennas can be performed using instruments made expressly for that purpose.

## Embrace Better Performance

– Unlock increased range

– Enhance signal clarity

– Improve overall reliability

– Maximize communication capabilities

Let's look at how choosing the right antenna gain is crucial to getting the best results after learning about a few common measurement methods.

**In order to get the best performance out of the antenna gain we choose, we need to take into account the following crucial factors:**

|  | Gain (dBi) | Range (Miles) | Signal Clarity | Reliability (%) |
|---|---|---|---|---|
| Antenna A | 10 | 50 | Satisfactory | 90 |
| Antenna B | 15 | 75 | Highly clear | 95 |
| Antenna C | 20 | 100 | Crystal clear | 98 |
| Antenna D | 25 | 125 | Exceptional | 99.5 |

It is evident from the above table that range, overall dependability, and signal quality are all directly impacted by antenna gain. By selecting an antenna with a larger gain, we can communicate with more individuals in our quest for improved performance. We can now look for even more effective techniques to improve antenna gain because we have a clear understanding of how to analyze antenna gain and how selecting the appropriate gain number may impact a system's performance.

## Increasing Gain in Antenna to Enhance Output

Let's go back to the previous section's discussion of selecting the ideal antenna gain and talk about how to maximize the antenna gain. For the purposes of this discussion, let's say that you upgraded the amateur radio station's signal reception by installing a high-gain Yagi antenna. Despite its outstanding specifications, you are not getting the expected boost in signal strength. To fix this and get the most out of your equipment, you'll need to learn how to raise radio gain. First, you might want to change the antenna's height and direction. Building an external antenna higher above the ground will help you get rid of anything that could be blocking the signals, including nearby buildings or foliage. Experimenting with different azimuth angles (turning the antenna so that it faces the opposite direction) can also significantly affect signal intensity by determining the best path to take the signal to the emitter. Second, by selecting the appropriate feedline lengths and plugs, you may minimize information loss in your transmitter, receiver, and antenna. Long-distance power supply can be provided with less noticeable loss when high-quality cables are used.

The performance of the system may be adversely affected by impedance mismatches, which can be avoided by using the proper connectors on both ends of the line. Lastly, by positioning active equipment nearby, such as preamplifiers or antenna amplifiers, you can further strengthen weak signals before they reach your receiver. By lowering potential noise during transmission over lengthy wire lines, these devices enhance signals that are received. To avoid adding too much noise or distortion to the received data, choosing the right amplification levels needs careful thought.

**To summarize these optimization techniques:**

- Changing the antenna's height and direction
- Using the right lead lengths and connections for the feedline
- Active devices for signal intensification are being added.

By carefully putting these recommendations into practice, you may optimize the advantages of your chosen high-gain antenna setup and enhance overall performance—longer range, sharper signals, and fewer interference.

| Optimization Technique | Benefits | Considerations |
| --- | --- | --- |
| Adjusting antenna height and orientation | Minimizes obstructions, improves range | Requires suitable mounting |
| Using proper feedline lengths and connectors | Reduces signal loss over distance | Select low-loss coaxial cables with matched connectors |
| Incorporating active devices during transmission | Amplifies weak signals, reduces noise selection | Careful amplification level |

By optimizing your antenna gain using these methods, you can significantly improve your amateur radio experience. Your time on amateur radio will be more enjoyable if you can increase your coverage since you will be able to talk more clearly and hear a greater range of bands.

# Knowledge of Antenna Polarization

One of the most important concepts in amateur radio is antenna polarization since it affects signal transmission and reception so greatly. A thorough understanding of radio polarization can be very helpful in promoting long-distance fan communication. Let us look at an amateur radio operator who lives in a highly populated area where electromagnetic pollution is present. This user may be able to improve their chances of getting a clean signal even in congested areas by carefully choosing the right antenna orientation. In amateur radio, antenna orientation is very important. It has to do with the electromagnetic radiation transmission and reception mechanisms of an antenna.

It is essential to comprehend how to receive and transmit information as efficiently as possible because antenna direction directly impacts communication efficiency. To further understand this idea, consider the following example: A transportable transceiver is being used to facilitate communication between two amateur radio operators. Operator A holds the receiver's antenna vertically so that it sticks out straight from the body. With their antenna pointed outward, Operator B positions theirs lateral to the body.

Due to their different orientation directions, individuals may encounter differences in signal strength and clarity.

- ❖ The direction of the antenna affects how well messages may be sent and received.
- ❖ Among the most popular radio orientation types are the circular, horizontal, and vertical ones.
- ❖ When the transmitting and receiving antennas have the same polarization, the system performs better.
- ❖ Weather fluctuations or interference from surrounding objects might change the antenna's direction.

You can also display specifics regarding antenna polarization using a table: When radio enthusiasts grasp the importance of antenna orientation, they may choose equipment with confidence. Information may go the farthest when the transmit and receive antennas are positioned correctly. Now that antenna polarization has practical applications, radio enthusiasts may understand them without having to specifically mention "step."

## Why is antenna polarization crucial for amateur radio?

In order to better understand the practical implications of antenna direction, let's look at a hypothetical situation. Let's say that Ben and Alex, two amateur radio operators, are utilizing small VHF radios to communicate from a hundred miles away. Both users are using the same channel and have identical antennas. Ben and Alex in this case originally configured their antennas to be vertically polarized. They quickly learn, though, that there is a noticeable signal loss and that their contact is quite crowded. They are so angry that they try to flip the antenna. Ben keeps his antenna pointed straight up, while Alex changes it so that it points horizontally. Suddenly, they are able to clearly and unobstructedly hear one other. This small adjustment improved the operation of their gearbox significantly. The significance of antenna direction for radio listeners is illustrated by this case study.

**You will be better able to understand the significance of antenna polarization if you have the following essential knowledge:**

There are four types of antenna polarization: vertical, horizontal, right- or left-handed. Antenna polarization is the direction of an antenna's electric field with respect to the ground. Antenna polarity has a major effect on the transmission's strength and quality. When the polarizations of the transmit and receive antennas are aligned, data travels more swiftly.

| Type | Advantages | Disadvantages |
|------|------------|---------------|
| Vertical | Omnidirectional pattern | Susceptible to noise |
| Horizontal | Reduced noise | Limited range |
| Circular RH | Better multipath | Lower gain |
| Circular LH | Improved satellite comms | Less common equipment |

Radio aficionados may choose and adjust their antenna polarizations with confidence if they understand these ideas and take into account real-world applications, as the one in our case study example.

## Differences in antenna polarization

Now let's look at some common antenna orientation setups found in home radio stations. **Armed with this information, you can choose the one that best suits your requirements.**

❖ **Vertical Polarization:** In this configuration, the radiating elements of the antennas are positioned vertically. When interacting with mobile or ground-based stations, like those on roads or highways, vertical polarization is frequently utilized. It works well for low-angle transmission, which makes it appropriate for long-distance communication over flat terrain.

❖ **Horizontal Polarization:** This orientation is preferred for line-of-sight communication between fixed stations at similar heights above the ground. It is particularly useful in urban areas where vertically polarized antennas may lose signal due to obstacles like buildings. Horizontal polarization antennas have their emitting parts positioned flat on the ground.

❖ **Circular Polarization:** This technique reduces multipath interference and improves simultaneous signal reception from several sources by rotating an electromagnetic wave's electric field vector around its axis while keeping it constant in magnitude.

Applications for circularly polarized antennas include mobile systems, satellite communications and areas where signal echoes and reflections are common. Depending on variables like obstructions, topography, and distance, different antenna orientations have distinct advantages. If you carefully explore these possibilities, you can increase the performance of your amateur radio system without having to make any changes. Now let's investigate the factors that influence antenna polarization effectiveness.

## Manipulating features for antenna polarization

As a continuation of our last section's explanation of the various types of antenna polarization frequently found in amateur radio sets, let's now address the variables that affect the choice of antenna polarization. Knowing this is important because, depending on the situation, it allows fans to engage with each other more deftly. Let us consider a hypothetical situation in which an amateur radio operator wants to speak with another operator hundreds of kilometers away. Since the selected frequency band is prone to solar flares and other natural events, it is known to contain a lot of background noise. In this case, minimizing signal loss and maximizing reception quality depend on choosing the right antenna orientation.

**There are four main sorts of objects that can change the direction of an antenna:**

- ❖ **Environmental Conditions:** Signal characteristics, like mountains or valleys, may impact line-of-sight communication and signal propagation. Vegetation density, like forests or urban areas, can attenuate or scatter radio waves, influencing signal quality. The presence of nearby buildings or structures can cause signal blockage or reflection, affecting signal strength and propagation.
- ❖ **Propagation Characteristics:** Radio wave propagation is affected by ionospheric conditions, which are impacted by sunspot activity and time of day. Atmospheric phenomena, such as refraction and scattering, can change the courses and strengths of signals.
- ❖ **Frequency Band Considerations:** Signal penetration via obstructions is determined by wavelength in relation to object size. Higher frequencies have trouble passing through obstacles; lower frequencies do. Different materials' signal absorption qualities influence signal attenuation, which in turn affects signal intensity and coverage.
- ❖ **System Requirements:** To provide sufficient signal coverage, antenna configuration and placement are determined by the required coverage area. In order to obtain adequate signal reception, antenna selection and orientation are influenced by the required signal intensity at receiver sites. To reduce signal deterioration, antenna design and placement are influenced by factors related to signal interference, such as co-channel interference or adjacent-channel interference.

Please refer to the table below for more information on how each of these factors affects the choice of antenna polarization:

| Category | Influence |
| --- | --- |
| Environmental | Nearby structures may cause multipath reflections leading to fading; vegetation affects signal loss |
| Propagation | Varying ionospheric conditions affect signals differently; scattering impacts overall signal quality |
| Frequency Band | Higher frequencies tend to require vertical polarization for efficient ground wave propagation |
| System Requirements | Directionality requirements affect choice; interference concerns may necessitate specific options |

Radio enthusiasts can choose their antenna orientation with confidence if they are aware of these characteristics. By carefully evaluating their arrangement, operators can increase the systems' dependability and communication range.

## How to determine the polarization of an antenna

We covered the importance of antenna polarization in amateur radio and how it could impact signal transmission in the previous section. Let's take a closer look at the many elements that affect antenna direction. Taking into account the working cadence is essential. For best results, different bands require different types of antennas with specific polarization orientations. For instance, vertically polarized antennas are commonly utilized in land-based rebroadcast systems and mobile communications due to the widespread use of VHF (Very High Frequency) and UHF (Ultra High Frequency) frequencies in these applications.

Another important factor to take into account is how close the object or structure is to it. The polarization characteristics of an antenna's broadcast pattern can be changed by reflections and multipath interference caused by trees, buildings, and even uneven terrain. Optimizing the position of your antenna requires a thorough understanding of your surroundings. The orientation of the polarization will also vary when the communication medium is changed due to the way electromagnetic waves behave. This idea is useful when traveling from space to items like cables and connectors. To achieve optimal transmission performance and avoid signal loss, the system must maintain uniform polarization throughout. Let's look at an example to see how these variables affect antenna polarization.

Assume, for example, that you are setting up an AM radio station in a neighborhood with plenty of big buildings. Presently:

- ❖ Tall buildings that are closely spaced have the ability to reflect messages with different polarizations.
- ❖ If changes are needed, tilting the vertical antennas slightly or looking into horizontally polarized antennas are other choices.
- ❖ Vertical antennas are particularly susceptible to multipath interference owing to echoes.
- ❖ Before installation, a thorough site investigation should be carried out to find any problems that can affect polarity.

Remember the following table while choosing the right antenna orientation for different situations:

| Scenario | Recommended Antenna Polarization |
|---|---|
| Urban areas with tall buildings | Horizontal |
| Open rural environments | Vertical |
| Mobile or portable operations | Circular (Omnidirectional) |
| Satellite communications or weak signals | Crossed (Circular/Linear) |

Lastly, those who appreciate radio listening ought to be aware of the variables affecting antenna direction. Signal travel can be improved by taking into account operating frequencies, the surroundings, and the properties of the communication medium.

## Antenna polarization applications in amateur radio

After talking about how to determine an antenna's polarization in the previous part, let's examine how antenna polarization is used in amateur radio. Consider the scenario when two operators are trying to communicate over great distances using basic VHF radios. This will demonstrate how crucial it is. Whereas Operator A's antenna is vertically polarized, Operator B's is horizontally polarized. Effective communication in these situations requires an understanding of how antenna polarization affects signal transmission.

The following are some crucial points to consider:

- ❖ **Signal strength:** The orientation of the antenna directly affects this, as it can either boost or weaken the received signal. When the transmitting and receiving antennas have the same polarization (horizontal to horizontal or vertical to vertical), the received signals are significantly stronger than when they are not.
- ❖ **Less interference:** Distinctly polarized antennas can lessen interference from surrounding sources sending obtrusive signals. This can improve communication overall and lessen disruptions during events or activities involving big groups of people.
- ❖ **Mitigating multipath fading:** Signals may be reflected off of buildings, the surroundings, or natural features. As a result, many signal lines may arrive at the listener concurrently and at different phases. Using antennas with diverse polarizations can assist address this problem because signals arriving from different directions may fade at different rates depending on their polarization?

When it comes to diversity reception, variety reception systems work best in difficult settings, like cities or places with frequently bad weather, when antennas with different polarizations are employed. These gadgets alternate between multiple antennas to find the strongest signal with the least amount of interference at any given time. This increases the system's dependability and range. To shed light on these real effects, Table 1 lists the numerous parameters that affect matching and mismatching antenna polarizations.

| Factor | Matching Polarizations | Mismatched Polarizations |
| --- | --- | --- |
| Signal strength | Stronger | Weaker |
| Interference reduction | Enhanced | Reduced |
| Multipath fading | Minimized | Increased |
| Diversity reception | Improved performance | Limited effectiveness |

In conclusion, radio enthusiasts who wish to communicate successfully and regularly can use antenna orientation in real-world scenarios. Operators can improve links across long distances or in difficult situations by taking into account signal strength, interference reduction, multipath fading avoidance, and diversity reception.

## DIY Exercises

1. Discuss some common types of antennas and how they function with Baofeng radios
2. Explain the classifications of Antenna Gain
3. What are the Factors Governing Antenna Gain?
4. Explain How to Choose the Best Antenna Gain
5. Why is antenna polarization crucial for amateur radio?
6. Explain How to determine the polarization of an antenna
7. Explain Antenna polarization applications in amateur radio

# CHAPTER SIX

# STEER CLEAR OF INTERRUPTIONS

## Finding and Fixing Interference

Follow these guidelines to locate and eliminate interferences:

- ❖ **Connect via USB:** To connect your radio to your computer, use a USB cable.
- ❖ **Start the CHIRP software:** Turn on your computer and start the CHIRP software.
- ❖ **Switch on the radio:** Make sure the radio is switched on and adjust the volume to full.
- ❖ **Download Radio Settings:** Connect your radio to your computer via USB by using the CHIRP software. Get your radio's current settings by downloading them.
- ❖ **Locate the Squelch Settings:** Look through the tabs or sections of the program to determine which ones have the squelch settings. You may find this under subsections such as "Settings" or "Service Settings."
- ❖ **Modify Squelch Ranges:** Enter the updated squelch ranges in the fields provided, for both VHF and UHF frequencies.
- ❖ **Upload Changes to Radio:** After making the required modifications, re-connect your radio via USB to your computer using the CHIRP program. Reload the updated configuration on your radio.
- ❖ **Test Functionality:** Test the mute settings to make sure they have been successfully adjusted. Verify that the squelch settings function as planned.
- ❖ **Repeat for Optimization:** If necessary, carry out the procedure again to adjust the parameters for best results.

## Monitoring the local legislation that are applicable

### Using a UV-5R to Monitor GMRS/FRS Data

At first, the FCC offered some clarifications. Family Radio Service (FRS), a private voice and data service, allows families and organizations to communicate over short distances. For short-range FRS channels, people most commonly use small handheld radios that look like walkie-talkies for back-and-forth communication. The following 22 channels, which are between 462 and 467 MHz, are available for usage by the FRS. All of them are accessible to the GMRS. There are a few differences between GMRS and FRS. The frequencies used by GMRS and FRS are the same, however GMRS provides extra functionality such faster data transfer and "short data messaging applications including text messaging and GPS location information." But obtaining a license will set you back seventy dollars. These frequencies are used by the walkie-talkies that you may buy from a big-box store. Nevertheless, these walkie-talkies frequently only show the channels—not the frequency.

Before we get started, let me just make one more very critical note: utilizing a Part 90 device, like the Baofeng UV-5R or any of its siblings, to broadcast on the FRS or GMRS frequencies is illegal. Although I haven't found any examples of the FCC behaving in this way, it's still something to be aware of. To be in compliance with the legislation, you must use a radio that has been approved under Part 95, like the Baofeng GMRS-V1 or any of the many pre-made solutions. Not only is it permissible to use things like channel bandwidth without a license, but I won't get into that because sending on a UV-5R is not something you should be doing. As before, CHIRP will be used to set the UV-5R to these frequencies. Now empty everything out and give it a thorough cleaning!

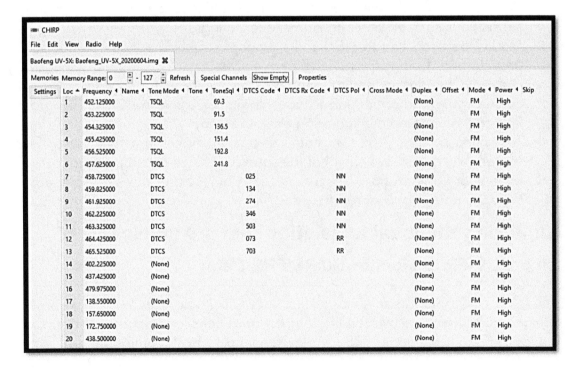

To move on to the next step, navigate to File > Open Stock Config > US FRS and GMRS Channels.

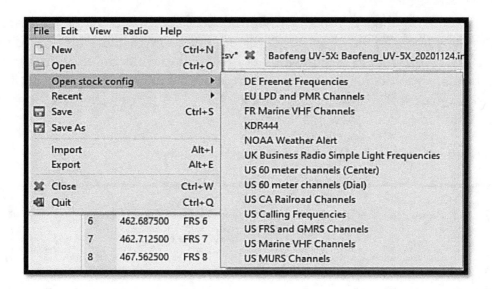

When it's open, it will appear like this.

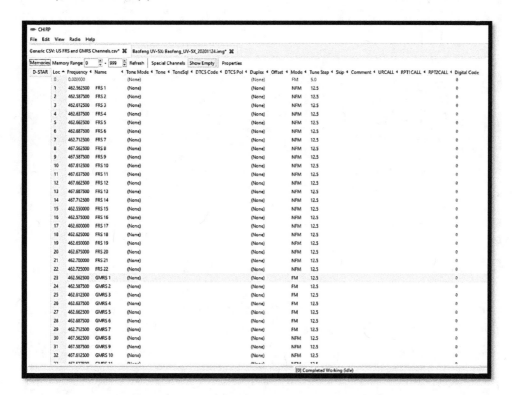

You can select channels FRS 1–22 from this website, copy them, and then include them in your UV-5R file. The UV-5r is unaffected by the Tune Step column, so don't worry about it. Maybe you've also noticed that on a couple of the frequencies, GMRS

1–22 is written. In theory, you don't need to duplicate these frequencies because they are the same. On the other hand, fifteen of the GMRS channels have different buffer sizes. If you want to be sure you hear everything, you can also paste them in. It's not necessary to do this, but it won't change what you hear. Minimum on the UV-5R. I had some problems with my Radioditty GD-77 after adjusting the bandwidth. The junk started to come over the speaker.

**This is what you will have at the end of it all.**

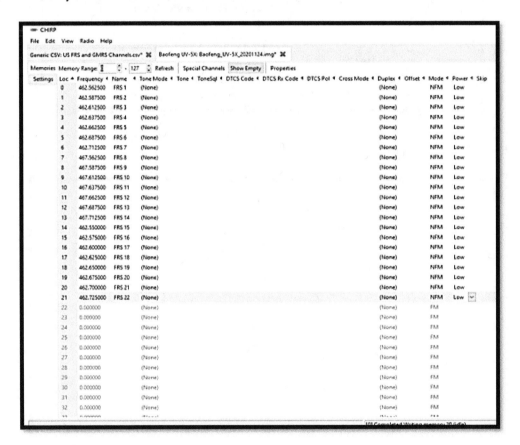

I think you should set all Power fields to Low in order to prevent accidentally sending something that exceeds FRS's power constraints. Anyway, because I don't think you should send anything, I would just off VHF/UHF TX in the Other Settings Menu.

| | | | |
|---|---|---|---|
| Memories | | Firmware Message 1: | HN5RV01 |
| Settings | Basic Settings | Firmware Message 2: | 1 |
| | Advanced Settings | 6+Power-On Message 1: | 151123H |
| | Other Settings | 6+Power-On Message 2: | |
| | Work Mode Settings | Power-On Message 1: | WELCOME |
| | FM Radio Preset | Power-On Message 2: | |
| | DTMF Settings | Power-On Message: | Message ⌄ |
| | Service Settings | VHF Lower Limit (MHz): | 130 |
| | | VHF Upper Limit (MHz): | 179 |
| | | VHF TX Enabled: | ☐ Enabled |
| | | UHF Lower Limit (MHz): | 400 |
| | | UHF Upper Limit (MHz): | 520 |
| | | UHF TX Enabled: | ☐ Enabled |

Furthermore, the duplex field can remain at 0 because they are all simplex channels. Lastly, connect your radio, save your picture file, and share it. Next, you can select A and B from the list of favorites by choosing VFO/MR on the radio. Holding down the * key will begin the scan. The A and B are useful if you want to monitor two frequencies where you are positive to detect activity, even if they are not required for screening.

Maybe you're wondering why I advised against adding any more tones. Nevertheless, they have no bearing whatsoever on tracking. You can hear all conversations on that frequency while your tone is set to none/CSQ, even if the sender isn't using a tone or "privacy code." They do nothing to safeguard privacy; all they do is let several users to share a single frequency. You can "capture" the tone if you'd like to know, but the UV-5R makes it difficult. The only method to keep your privacy on a radio is to use encryption, which isn't supported here. Finally, any discussion conducted over FRS/GMRS (or any other unencrypted channel) can be overheard by everyone.

Once you've set your UV-5R to the FRS/GMRS frequency, you may be interested in what you can hear and how far away something is. Depending on your location, the type of antenna you have, and the radios being utilized, your response to that question will vary. If you're at a city protest, you might be able to hear someone using an FRS/GMRS radio within a few blocks of you, depending on how strong their signal is. The FCC states that an FRS device's typical range between channels 8 and 14 is less than half a mile. Depending on the circumstances, there may be larger gaps between contacts on channels 1 through 7 and between 15 and 22. Naturally, depending on who, if anyone, is listening to the radio, what you hear will alter. I found it really amazing to hear children conversing with one another in the comfort of their own homes as I was testing one of my antennas. You might not experience the same results. A few remarks regarding GMRS. The signal wills most likely reach farther if someone is using a radio with higher transmit power and GMRS capability. However, they must sign their name at the beginning and finish of each program, as well as at least once every ten minutes. Every callsign is distinct and serves to identify a certain individual. Remember to give your name if you are using a radio that recognizes GMRS licenses! It is possible that no one with a UV-5R is using the FRS/GMRS frequencies.

They may be using MURS or the 2-meter/70-centimeter public radio frequency, if they have a license. MURS can be found in the File -> Open Stock Config menu's US MURS Channels section. Setting it up is not too difficult. Additionally, there are the National Calling Frequencies (Ham Simplex) for 70 centimeters and two meters. According to the ARRL band planning, single frequencies are located between 146.40 and 146.58 MHz and 147.42 and 147.57 MHz. You could even check out the band plans for your local radio club and program in their simplex frequencies if that still concerns you. However, it is doubtful that these frequencies will be used by unauthorized users. Now, you may listen in on the FRS and GMRS frequencies using a UV-5R or any other radio that is CHIRP-compatible. Look for a link to the picture file in this section that has every frequency listed so you may put it into your UV-5R with ease.

## Understanding Scanning

The Baofeng UV-82 has an inbuilt reader that operates on both VHF and UHF bands. The scanner adjusts frequencies in accordance with the selected frequency step while it is in frequency (VFO) mode. In contrast, when it is in Channel (MR) mode, it moves through the saved channels. Holding down the [SCAN] button for about two seconds will activate the scanner. To exit the scanning process, press any button. The scanner can be used in three distinct ways: Time, Carrier, and Search. Use these steps to modify the reader setting.

## How to Modify the Mode of the Scanner

❖ To access the menu, use the [MENU] button.
❖ Enter [1] [8] on the number keyboard, which corresponds to the reader mode choice.
❖ To ensure your choice is correct, press the [MENU] button.
❖ The numerous reading methods can be accessed by using the [UP] and [DOWN] keys.
❖ To preserve your selected reading strategy, click the [MENU] button.
❖ To close the page and go back to the main menu, click the [EXIT] button.

**Let's now examine the different scanning modes:**

❖ **Time Operation (TO):** When a signal is detected, the scanner stops scanning in Time Operation mode. Regardless of whether the signal is still present or not, it resumes scanning after a certain amount of time.
❖ **Carrier Operation (CO):** When a signal is detected, the scanner stops searching and stays inactive until the signal goes away. It doesn't start scanning again until the signal is lost.
❖ **Search Operation (SE):** This mode operates in a manner akin to that of Time Operation mode. The scanner stops scanning and waits when it finds a signal in this mode. After a predetermined amount of time, it starts scanning again whether or not the signal is still present.

If you would want to scan again in any of these modes, hold down the [SCAN] button for a while longer. These modes provide a range of features that are specifically designed to meet specific needs. This enables users to adjust the functionality of the scanner to meet their needs and the requirements of their communication duties.

# About Tone scanning

When your Baofeng radio is in frequency mode, you can use the following methods to search busy frequencies for CTCSS (Continuous Tone-Coded Squelch System) tones or DCS (Digital-Coded Squelch) codes.

## Methods for Performing Tone Scanning

1. Press the [MENU] button to access the menu.
2. Use the number pad to enter one of the following numbers:
   - Type [1] [0] to initiate a search for DCS codes.
   - Alternatively, press [1] [1] to start searching for CTCSS sub-tones.
3. Press the [MENU] button to confirm your selection.
4. Briefly press the [SCAN] button to initiate the scanning process.
5. As the radio begins scanning, you'll see "CT" or "DCS" flashing on the monitor. This indicates that the radio is detecting the tone or code.
6. While scanning, the radio will emit a beep and stop flashing when it identifies a tone or code.
7. Press the [SCAN] button to confirm the detected tone or code.
8. Finally, press the [EXIT] button to exit the menu and return to the previous screen.

You can actively search for and identify certain DCS codes or CTCSS tones that are in use on available frequencies by using this strategy. You can discover and detect these signaling codes with your Baofeng radio to the fullest extent possible by following these procedures. Using these code or tone settings, you can use this to monitor situations or configure your radio to communicate with other people.

# The System of Dual Reception and Dual Watch

Despite having just one antenna, the Baofeng UV-82 radio's Dual Watch feature allows users to simultaneously listen to two stations. This function increases the conversation's versatility by enabling the gadget to automatically switch between two frequencies on a regular basis. It's crucial to understand that for the feature to work while the phone is in Dual Watch mode, a few features are disabled.

## Features Not Provided in Dual Watch Configuration

- ❖ Reverse operation
- ❖ **Channel mode:** using the [POUND] button to toggle between high and low transmission powers
- ❖ Duplex channel saving

Follow these steps to adjust the setup and turn on or off the Dual Watch mode:

## How to Turn Dual Watch Mode on and Off

❖ To enter the menu, press [MENU]; to access Dual Watch, press [7] on the number pad.

❖ Press the [MENU] button to choose this option.
❖ To turn on or off the Dual Watch mode, press and hold the [UP] and [DOWN] buttons.

❖ To confirm that you want to choose, press [MENU].
❖ Click [EXIT] to close this window.

The radio in Dual Watch mode may transmit on either channel A or channel B, depending on which channel activates first. Having stated that, there may be a problem if the device is unable to send because of the current frequency. To fix this, you can choose to lock the radio to either channel A or channel B.

To make use of this feature, take the following actions:

## Actions to Take: Locking the Dual Watch Transmit Channel

- ❖ **Getting to the Menu:** To begin, hit the [MENU] button to bring up the menu on the radio.
- ❖ **Choosing TDR-AB:** Enter [3] [4] on the number keypad, which corresponds to the TDR-AB choice. After entering, make sure your option is correct by pressing the [MENU] button.
- ❖ **Toggling Between Screens A and B:** After choosing TDR-AB, you can use the keypad's [UP] and [DOWN] keys to alternate between screens A and B.
- ❖ **Verifying Your Selection:** Click the [MENU] button to indicate that you wish to go from screen A to screen B.
- ❖ **Leaving the Page:** Lastly, use the [EXIT] button to go back to the previous screen or main menu from the TDR-AB settings page.

You can press the [PTT-A] or [PTT-B] button first, then the [PTT] button to momentarily deactivate the lock without exiting the menu. These features provide customers more control over the Dual Watch mode on the Baofeng UV-82 radio by letting them alter the broadcast settings and guarantee smooth and quick connection.

## DIY Exercises

1. Discuss some guidelines to locate and eliminate interferences
2. What do you understand by Scanning
3. Discuss the Methods for Performing Tone Scanning
4. Mention some Features Not Provided in Dual Watch Configuration
5. Explain How to Turn Dual Watch Mode on and Off

# CHAPTER SEVEN

# INSIGHTS INTO MILITARY COMMUNICATION

## Comprehending Discussions in Military Groups

Military letters Military radios are a subclass of Baofeng radios that are intended and utilized for military purposes. Under the Baofeng brand, a variety of radios are manufactured, like as walkie-talkies, portable transceivers, and amateur radios. Baofeng offers radios that are specifically made to meet the needs of military use, even though their versions are also commonly used for residential and recreational purposes. Military Baofeng radios, which are ruggedized to withstand the kind of harsh handling and extreme conditions typical of military applications, are typically used for these communications. They might also contain advanced encryption and security technologies to offer secure communication channels. Military-grade Baofeng radios often have greater transmission power and longer battery life to enable longer field operations. Additionally, military communication is crucial. Tactic channel scanning, compatibility with military-specific frequencies and protocols, and interoperability with other military communication systems are examples of specialized features of Baofeng radios. These qualities are necessary for military personnel to communicate successfully in a variety of operational contexts, including combat operations, training exercises, and emergency response scenarios. Reliable portable radios are crucial for emergency communications. Let's explore the world of Baofeng radios and look at a few choices for those seeking more powerful and sophisticated alternatives to the popular Baofeng UV-5R.

## Baofeng UV-5R: A Typical Option

The Baofeng UV-5R and its sibling model, the F8HP, are well-liked choices because to their affordability and versatility. It's important to recognize that there are better solutions available, though.

Consider the following aspects while choosing a portable radio:

❖ **Accessibility:** Is it easy to obtain the radio from retailers? Finding some variants in perfect condition becomes more challenging because they might only be available as military or law enforcement surplus.
❖ **Interoperability:** Can this radio communicate with other radios of different makes and models? Ensuring compatibility can help reach a larger number of people in an emergency.

❖ **Adoption Ease:** Consider the learning curve associated with the radio. Certain models can require more user assistance than others.

**Let's now examine various potentials**

❖ **Baofeng AR-152:** This 10W ham radio has a powerful dual-band, long-range antenna in addition to tactical functions. For modification, a 12,000mAh battery and a programming cable are included. Due to its strong construction, it is suitable for emergencies.
❖ **Alternatives:** Look at radios like the Yaesu FT-60R, Kenwood TH-D74A, or Icom IC-2730A if you want to go beyond Baofeng. These radios have improved interoperability, build quality, and usefulness.

Recall that during emergencies, communication is essential. Make sensible decisions, get comfortable with your radio, and make sure you have a network of other communicators available in case you need to communicate.

# Creating Effective Communication Techniques

A few crucial components must be carefully considered when creating a military communication plan with Baofeng radios in order to guarantee dependability, security, and interoperability under a range of operating conditions.

**Below is a high-level summary of the actions and things to think about:**

❖ **Know the Equipment:** To guarantee that Baofeng radios are used effectively in a variety of situations, familiarize yourself with their features and capabilities.
❖ **Creating Communication Protocols:** Create explicit communication protocols that include frequency distribution, established call signs, and encryption requirements. Employees should have training to guarantee that these guidelines are followed for structured, safe communication.
❖ **Interoperability:** To improve interoperability and enable smooth communication between various units, program Baofeng radios to be interoperable with other equipment used by emergency services or allied forces.
❖ **Security Measures:** Use frequency-hopping and encryption to protect sensitive data and communications that are essential to the mission from jamming and eavesdropping.
❖ **Emergency readiness:** To ensure prompt and efficient reaction in times of distress, include emergency channels and signals in the communication plan.

This will improve the plan's overall disaster readiness and response capabilities.

- ❖ **Maintenance and Support:** To guarantee optimum performance and dependability when required, set up a system for routine maintenance inspections and troubleshooting assistance for the radios.
- ❖ **Exercise and Drills:** Hold frequent drills to hone communication under a range of circumstances, including hacked ones. Employees get more comfortable with procedures and gain confidence in their ability to use the radios efficiently as a result.
- ❖ **Review and Adaptation:** To make sure the communication plan is current and useful over time and enhances overall communication effectiveness, review it frequently and make adjustments based on input and shifting operational requirements.

Remember that having the right people in place who can operate the technology under pressure is just as crucial to the success of military communication as having the right tools. It takes constant training and practice to keep communication as a dependable lifeline in any situation.

**Let's dissect this step-by-step tutorial further and provide straightforward explanations for each step:**

- ❖ **First, Determine Your Communication Needs:** Before rushing into setting up communication solutions, it's imperative to understand what your team or business requires. Making decisions on which communication tools to employ and where is part of this. Consider aspects such as the working environment, the distance between team members, and the necessary frequency of communication.
- ❖ **Choose the Right Instruments:** Having assessed your communication needs, the next step is to select the right technologies. While we are talking about Baofeng radios here, any type of communication equipment could be employed. Verify that the radios you choose have the functionality, frequency, and range that you require. Remember to get all necessary accessories, including antennas, batteries, and chargers, to guarantee your radios operate as intended.
- ❖ **Create Standard Operating Procedures (SOPs) in Step Three:** You need to have clear instructions on how to use your radios in order to facilitate effective communication. SOPs outline how to handle crises, exchange information (call signals), and decide which frequencies to use. These procedures ensure

that everyone is on the same page and knows what to do in different situations.

- ❖ **Employee Training:** Even the best instruments are useless if people cannot operate them. Plan training sessions to teach everyone the proper handling and operation of the radios. It's also a good idea to run drills to make sure that everyone feels comfortable using the radios, especially in high-stress situations.

- ❖ Program Radios Now is the time to make the necessary changes to your radios' settings. This also involves setting the right encryption keys and frequency, if needed. It is essential to verify the radios after programming to ensure everything is working properly before using them.

- ❖ **Put Security Measures in Place:** To protect sensitive data, you must secure your communication connections. You must utilize encryption and other security methods to prevent unauthorized access to your transmissions. It's also essential to keep up with security standards in order to stay ahead of any threats.

- ❖ **Establish Upkeep Schedules:** To ensure that your communication equipment stays in top working condition, you must do routine maintenance. This entails assigning certain people to manage upkeep and repairs as well as organizing routine inspections to spot issues before they become serious.

- ❖ **Determine Interoperability:** When working with other teams or organizations, it's imperative to make sure that your communication systems can work together as a cohesive entity. Make sure your radios are compatible with theirs and coordinate communication protocols to avoid misunderstandings.

- ❖ **Carry Out Field Training:** To test your communication plan, run field exercises that simulate real-world situations. This gives you valuable feedback for future development and enables you to evaluate the resilience of your communication systems to stress.

- ❖ **Review and Revise:** Finally, evaluate your communication strategy on a regular basis to identify areas for improvement. This could involve introducing new technology, adapting your plan based on feedback from drills, or making adjustments to your operating environment. You can ensure the long-term functionality of your communication systems by being flexible and willing to make changes.

# In-Depth Analysis of the Factors That Determine Effective Military Communication

- ❖ **Objectivity:** Clear, concise, and unambiguous communication is required. Clear communication ensures that instructions or information are understood accurately and reduces the chance of misunderstandings.
- ❖ **Brevity:** Military communication usually needs to be concise due to time constraints and the need for prompt responses. It is possible to communicate more quickly and efficiently by speaking plainly and leaving out subtleties.
- ❖ **Accuracy:** Information transmitted by Baofeng radios must be reliable and accurate. Inaccurate information can lead to costly errors or misinterpretations, especially in emergency situations.
- ❖ **Timeliness:** To ensure that messages are received when needed, it's critical to communicate as soon as possible. Operational effectiveness and mission success can be negatively impacted by communication delays.
- ❖ **Security:** When it comes to military communication using Baofeng radios, security must come first. Secure communication protocols and encryption help protect sensitive data from prying eyes and surveillance.
- ❖ **Adaptability:** Military operations are sometimes abrupt and dynamic. Plans for communication should be adaptable enough to take into account changing circumstances, allowing for quick adjustments and backup plans when needed.
- ❖ **Hierarchy:** When a clear communication hierarchy is in place, messages are transmitted through the appropriate channels and reach the appropriate parties. Because of its hierarchical structure, command and control are easier maintained in complex military environments.
- ❖ **Rehearsal:** Practicing communication procedures through drills and exercises improves the effectiveness and efficiency of actual operations. It is less likely for errors to be made under pressure when communication standards are understood.
- ❖ **Feedback:** Communication protocols can be continuously enhanced by implementing feedback mechanisms. It is simpler to identify areas that require optimization and improvement when staff feedback is gathered via Baofeng radios.
- ❖ **Training:** All participants must receive the required instruction in the use of Baofeng radios and communication protocols. Operators are ensured to be proficient with radio use, compliance with communication protocols, and problem-solving techniques through training.

## DIY Exercises

1. What do you understand by Discussions in Military Groups?
2. What are the aspects to consider while choosing a portable Baofeng UV-5R radio?
3. What are the actions to take in Creating Effective Communication Techniques?
4. Discuss the In-Depth Analysis of the Factors That Determine Effective Military Communication

# CHAPTER EIGHT
# COMMUNICATION TECHNIQUES IN AN EMERGENCY

Emergency communication strategies must make use of Baofeng radios' capacity to facilitate effective communication during crises.

**In an emergency, Baofeng radios can be utilized specifically for the purposes listed below:**

- ❖ **Pre-programmed Channels:** Configure Baofeng radios to communicate exclusively through emergency channels.
- ❖ **Backup Power:** Make sure Baofeng radios are equipped with backup power sources, such as extra batteries or external power banks, to ensure that communication is maintained during prolonged power outages or emergencies. These channels should be set up, especially for vital communication during emergencies, free of any non-essential traffic.
- ❖ **Emergency frequencies:** Acquire knowledge of the emergency frequencies related to your region or jurisdiction. These frequencies are usually reserved for emergency services, and during an emergency, they can be monitored for important updates and instructions.
- ❖ **Dual-Band operating:** Monitor multiple frequency bands simultaneously by utilizing Baofeng radios' dual-band operating function. This allows you to stay informed about changes on many channels, such as emergency services, public safety, and amateur radio frequencies.
- ❖ **Simplex Communication:** When repeaters or other infrastructure may be unavailable or compromised, use the simplex communication mode on Baofeng radios. Because simplex communication allows direct radio-to-radio communication without the need for an intermediary infrastructure, it is ideal for emergency situations.
- ❖ **Emergency Codes and Signals:** Create and disseminate emergency codes and signals that can be utilized to quickly and surreptitiously use Baofeng radios to send vital information. The types of emergencies, their priorities, and the actions that first responders should take can all be specified by these codes.
- ❖ **Fast Deployment Kits:** Assemble packages with extra batteries, antennas, Baofeng radios, and other required equipment for speedy deployment. These

kits need to be readily deployable and accessible to critical personnel and response teams in the event of an emergency.

- ❖ **Exercise and training:** Organize regular training sessions and emergency communication drills to familiarize users with the operation, protocol, and procedures of Baofeng radios. Practice scenarios involving distress calls, resource coordination, and transmitting critical information to improve readiness for actual emergencies.
- ❖ **Arrangements with Outside Organizations:** Establish communication channels and protocols to enable collaboration with other entities, such as law enforcement, emergency services, and government agencies. Make sure that the Baofeng radios and other communication technologies these agencies use are interoperable in order to foster effective communication and cooperation.
- ❖ **Education and Public Awareness:** Disseminate information regarding the necessity of Baofeng radios for communication and readiness during emergencies. People should be taught and trained in emergency procedures, basic radio use, and the importance of clear and concise communication during emergencies.

## Digital Procedures in Case of Emergencies

When digital protocols are used, Baofeng radios perform significantly more effectively and dependably in emergency situations.

Important digital protocols that are commonly employed in emergency situations include the following:

- ❖ **Digital Mobile Radio (DMR):** This digital radio technology makes voice and data transmission possible. It has advantages over analog systems, including as greater coverage, longer battery life, and improved audio quality. DMR-compatible Baofeng radios enable dependable communication in emergency situations.
- ❖ **NXDN:** NXDN is a digital narrowband protocol that aims to optimize bandwidth use. It is appropriate for essential communications in emergency response scenarios since it can transfer both data and audio. Baofeng radios with NXDN capability ensure clear and safe communication in challenging environments.
- ❖ **Project 25 (P25):** P25 is a collection of digital radio standards intended for public safety and emergency services. It enables interoperable contact

between many agencies and ensures encrypted and reliable communication using Baofeng radios during crises.

❖ **Digital Private Mobile Radio (dPMR):** dPMR is a digital protocol intended for low-power portable radios. Baofeng radios are useful for emergency communication because they provide secure communication, efficient spectrum utilization, and advanced features like text messaging and GPS tracking.

❖ **Digital Mobile Radio Tier II (DMR-Tier II):** Two-way radios that support digital voice and data transfer employ the DMR Tier II standard. Baofeng radios that adhere to DMR Tier II provide features including data transfer, individual and group calling, and better coordination and collaboration during emergencies.

❖ **Digital Emergency System (DES):** DES is a digital protocol that was created to provide priority to emergency communications. Baofeng radios with DES capability can prioritize emergency signals over non-essential communications in an emergency, ensuring that they are immediately attended to.

❖ **Digital Encryption:** Many digital protocols include encryption for secure communication in sensitive situations. Baofeng radios with digital encryption safeguard private information and prevent unauthorized access to communication channels during emergencies.

When utilizing Baofeng radios in emergency situations, it is essential to choose the right digital protocol based on compatibility, coverage needs, and security requirements to ensure dependable and efficient communication between reaction teams and stakeholders.

# Recognizing the Vital Communication Frequencies for Survival

The key to making the most of your Baofeng radio for survival communication is to familiarize yourself with its principal frequencies and radio services. Knowing these expressions can help you select the right frequencies for your needs and situation. MURS, or Multi-Use Radio Service 151.820, 151.880, 151.940, 154.570, and 154.600 MHz are the MURS frequencies. The Multi-Use Radio Service (MURS) is a reconfigurable group of VHF (Very High Frequency) channels designed for short-range general-purpose communication.

Among the notable characteristics of MURS are:

- ❖ **License-Free:** MURS channels allow the general public to utilize them without obtaining an FCC license, making them an accessible choice for immediate communication. But even when utilizing a Baofeng radio, a HAM radio operator's license is still needed.
- ❖ **Five Channels:** MURS offers five distinct VHF channels, each with a special purpose.
- ❖ These channels are ideal for individual and small-group communication tasks like setting up neighborhood watch programs or staying in touch while going on outdoor expeditions.
- ❖ **Short to Medium Range:** MURS channels, which typically provide dependable communication within a 1-3 mile radius, can be helpful for local coordination in our 2-mile radius area. However, the range may vary depending on obstructions and terrain.

## Family Radio Service (FRS): An Overview

The FRS frequencies are 462.5625 - 462.725 MHz. A UHF (Ultra High Frequency) radio service called the Family Radio Service (FRS) is intended for close-quarters communication between small groups and families.

Essential elements of FRS comprise:

- ❖ **License-Free:** Similar to MURS, FRS channels are open to the public and do not require a license, making them accessible to casual users. But even when utilizing a Baofeng radio, a HAM radio operator's license is still needed.
- ❖ **Twenty-Two Channels:** FRS offers a total of 22 channels for communication, offering a variety of channel options. These channels are widely used for communication at theme parks, hiking, and camping, among other outdoor activities.
- ❖ **Short Range:** For short-range communication, an FRS radio's typical range is one to two miles. Its range may be impacted by the obstructions and terrain.

## The GMRS, known as General Mobile Radio Service

GMRS operates between 462.550 and 467.725 MHz. A feature-rich UHF radio service with increased capability and communication range is called General Mobile Radio Service (GMRS).

Key elements of GMRS include:

- ❖ **License Required:** Unlike MURS and FRS, GMRS requires users to acquire an FCC license, which protects their family or group. This license increases the sending power and communication range while granting access to repeaters. But even when utilizing a Baofeng radio, a HAM radio operator's license is still needed.
- ❖ **Fifteen Channels:** Including the channels shared with FRS, GMRS offers fifteen channels in total. This allows you to select the channel that most effectively meets your specific communication needs.
- ❖ **Extended Range:** When repeaters are utilized, GMRS radios can have a range of more than five miles, in contrast to MURS and FRS.
- ❖ It's true that BAOFENG only possesses GMRS radios. An FCC license is still required, but testing is not required. This is a fantastic choice for anyone looking for a trustworthy communication tool without a HAM radio license.

# Communication Strategies to Use in an Emergency Situation

## How to Dial a Standard Emergency Number

Practically, you may start using the UV-5R right now. Turn it on, choose a basic broadcast station, and tune in to that frequency. It is quite easy to use. Let's keep things basic as this is probably your first time using radio. Prior to making any adjustments, "Zero Out" or turn the radio back on. Ensure that the battery pack is firmly attached to the transceiver's back. After the antenna is fastened to the antenna post, tighten it. To turn on the radio, turn the volume knob counterclockwise. The radio will beep twice before a voice says, "Channel Mode" or "Frequency Mode." Pro Tip: **To ensure that no preset settings are obstructing emergency communications, "zero out" (reset) the radio to its original settings:**

- ❖ To access the menu, press the radio's MENU key.
- ❖ Find Menu Option 40: Scroll through the menu options by using the keypad's up and down arrow buttons until you find option 40.
- ❖ Choose "ALL": Press the MENU button once more to select "ALL."
- ❖ Select "SOURCE?" Press the MENU button a third time.
- ❖ Turn the Radio Back On: To turn the radio back on and to exit the menu, press the MENU button four times.

**To select the language of your choice:**
- ❖ To access the menu, press the radio's MENU key.
- ❖ **Locate Option 14:** Use the arrow keys to navigate through the menu selections until you reach option 14.

- ❖ **Select a Different Language:** To access the language selection submenu, press the MENU button once again.
- ❖ **Choose Your Language:** Press the arrow keys to go to the English (or other language of your choice) "ENG" option.
- ❖ **Verify Language Selection:** To verify your language choice, press the MENU button one again.
- ❖ **Exit:** Press the MENU key to end the menu.

## Employ UV-5R's FM radio

During emergencies, local radio stations may play emergency alerts and educational programs. You can use the UV-5R as a simple FM radio by setting the station to your preferred frequency. Simply press the orange "CALL" button on the radio to switch to FM mode. Furthermore, you can reach any station by continuously holding down the */"SCAN" key. Insert the emergency frequency, carry it with you, and make use of it. After selecting a frequency, you can begin sending and receiving by tapping the appropriate keypad numbers. For example, typing 162.400 will direct you to the NOAA weathercast. Alternatively, you can reach the main national emergency line by dialing 151.940. We won't have to memorize every frequency number in case of an emergency.

**Use these procedures to store a frequency and establish a new channel:**

- ❖ To put the radio in Frequency (VFO) Mode, press VFO/MR.
- ❖ Once you have selected the top frequency by pressing the A/B button, you will see an arrow to the left of the frequency on the screen to show that you have done so.
- ❖ The upper frequency must be used in all programming.
- ❖ **Turn off TDR and Dual Standby (be sure; it should be deactivated by now).**
  - ✓ Press the menu icon.
  - ✓ Hit the 7.
  - ✓ Press MENU to select the item from the menu.
  - ✓ Select "OFF" with the up and down arrows.
  - ✓ Press Menu to verify.
  - ✓ Then Exit
- ❖ Using the keypad, enter the frequency you want to save.
- ❖ Select MENU from the menu.
- ❖ Pick option 27.
- ❖ Press MENU again to view the channel list.

❖ A channel already has a frequency recorded if "CH-" appears before the channel number. To choose the desired channel (000 to 127), press the up and down arrows.
❖ To store the frequency to the chosen channel, press the MENU key.
❖ Then Exit

Every channel in the list of saved frequencies will be played on the radio; to choose a saved frequency, press the up and down arrows and VFO/MR to enter channel mode. Two saved frequencies and the channel on which each frequency is saved will be shown on the screen when in channel mode.

## DIY Exercises

1. Explain the purposes that the Baofeng radios can specifically serve in case of an emergency
2. Discuss the important digital protocols that are commonly employed in emergency situations
3. Explain Family Radio Service and its key elements
4. Explain General Mobile Radio Service and its key elements
5. Discuss the Communication Strategies to Use in an Emergency Situation
6. What are the procedures to store a frequency and establish a new channel?

# CHAPTER NINE

# THE BLOCK FREQUENCY VALIDATION

## Using a Wave Chart to Choose Which Frequencies to Block

The capacity to deliberately block frequencies is one of the most important skills for reducing the cacophony of electromagnetic waves surrounding us when it comes to radio transmissions. One of the most important things you can do to improve your radio scene is to decide which frequencies you want to block. This is crucial for radio enthusiasts who want to keep a strong signal, government organizations that want to ensure that everyone abides by the rules and businesses who want to protect critical data. Here, we'll talk about how to find and look into frequencies that need to be blocked while being mindful of the legal issues that come up in this complex field.

### Analyzing and Determining Block Frequencies

❖ It is required to conduct research and look for frequency databases in order to restrict frequencies. When Frequency Databases: Make use of comprehensive frequency databases kept up to date by governmental or business associations. These databases include important details regarding license holders, assignments, and frequencies that are licensed. For instance, the Federal Communications Commission (FCC) Frequency Database in the US and the Radio Spectrum Management website in New Zealand are both valuable sources of information.

❖ Invest in scanner and spectrum analyzer instruments to find frequencies that are being utilized actively in your area by scanning the radio spectrum. These instruments facilitate identification by offering up-to-date data on modulation, frequency, and signal strength.

❖ **Cooperation with Regulatory agencies:** Gain knowledge about frequency assignments, license requirements, and potential interference issues by collaborating with legal and regulatory agencies. They can offer guidance on frequencies that can be dangerous or legally questionable.

❖ **Frequency Monitoring Software:** To keep track of and record radio frequencies in your area, use specialist frequency monitoring software. By assisting in the identification of patterns and trends, these software tools guarantee adherence to radio rules and regulations. They are especially helpful to businesses that are trying to follow the law.

## Considerations for Legal Matters When Blocking Channels

❖ **Permissions and licenses.** It is crucial to ascertain your legal authority before proceeding and discontinuing any frequency. A significant portion of radio frequencies are assigned and licensed by government agencies. You risk legal repercussions if you tamper with legally approved broadcasts. It is important to always make sure you have the necessary permissions or permits before blocking any specific frequency.

❖ **Safety and Emergency Services:** Several frequencies have been set aside expressly to help with communication between emergency services and the general public. When certain frequencies are disabled, it may endanger public safety and have unfavorable effects. These essential routes must be protected at all costs, and legal requirements must be followed to guarantee their security.

❖ **Interference Mitigation:** It is necessary to restrict frequencies in order to limit interference, which is a legitimate goal. It's crucial to remember that all of this has to be done in accordance with the law. In order to avoid unintentional infractions, certain countries could require you to coordinate your activities with regulatory authorities to minimize interference.

❖ **Concerning security and privacy:** Blocking frequencies is a smart concept to preserve the privacy and safety of conversations. This will aid in preserving security and privacy. Nonetheless, it is crucial to be informed about any applicable privacy laws or regulations. Legal issues may arise from listening in on conversations or squelching frequencies without permission.

## The Blocked Frequencies arrangement

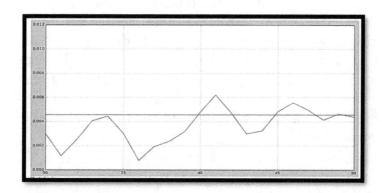

In the complex realm of radio transmission, programming and handling blocked frequencies is similar to using a conductor's baton to build a symphony. The process is extremely laborious and requires precision, a keen eye for detail, and familiarity with the intricate relationships between hardware and software. We will now discuss configuring prohibited frequencies with the incredibly versatile CHIRP program. We will emphasize how important accuracy is to this process.

## Detailed Instructions on Blocking with CHIRP Frequencies Added

❖ **Start CHIRP:** Turn on your computer and make sure that the programming wire that came with your Baofeng radio is compatible with it before starting the CHIRP application. Your radio will receive the programmed frequencies through this cable.

❖ **Download from Radio:** Open CHIRP's "Radio" menu, then choose "Download From Radio." This will pull up the most recent settings from your Baofeng radio, which you may examine and edit as necessary.

❖ **Select Which Frequencies to Block:** Decide which frequencies you want to stop. These can be undesired transmissions or signals that interfere. Take note of these frequencies so you have them handy.

❖ **Input Frequencies:** Click on the channel in CHIRP where you wish to add a filtered frequency. In case the cell bears the label "Frequency" or "Rx Frequency," type the frequency that you want to prevent. Make that the frequency is appropriately typed in megahertz (MHz) and that the decimal point is in the right place.

❖ **Modify Channel parameters:** As needed, modify the tone delay, broadcast frequencies, and channel names, among other channel parameters, according on your needs. Make sure you have these parameters set up to meet your requirements.

❖ **Repeat for Every Frequency:** Make a distinct channel for every frequency you want to block if you have more than one. Precise control over the blocked frequencies is made possible by this level of detail.

❖ **Transfer to Radio:** After configuring and adding all needed frequencies, transfer the updated configuration to your Baofeng radio. To block the designated frequencies, navigate to the "Radio" menu in CHIRP and choose "Upload to Radio." CHIRP will then send the new configuration to your radio.

# Testing and Verifying the Frequency Blocking

It is important that you manage and protect your frequencies in order to maintain the security of your stronghold. Your communication network accuracy is vital, and it could be brought down by any weak point. We are about to embark on a journey that requires both technological prowess and an uncompromising dedication to hermetic security. Our journey will formally commence when we attempt to confirm the frequency blocking on your Baofeng radio.

## Describe the Frequency Blocking Testing Procedure

❖ The first step in testing your Baofeng radio is to start a frequency shutdown. After you have specified the frequencies you wish to block into your Baofeng radio using the CHIRP application, this is required. You must set up your radio so that it prevents you from using the prohibited frequencies in order to achieve this.

❖ To make sure that the blocked frequencies can no longer be accessed, a transmission test should be run. Try sending or receiving messages on the frequencies that you have marked as forbidden in advance. If your frequency blocking setup is working correctly, you should either hear total silence or get an error message saying "access is denied".

❖ You can use the features or tools included into your Baofeng radio for signal tracking if you want to look for unwanted or blocked frequencies. Keep an eye on the radio spectrum to make sure that no illegal broadcasts or messages are using the frequencies that have been reserved for that specific purpose. If there is activity on these frequencies, more research needs to be done.

❖ To make sure the frequencies you have marked as prohibited are still not being used, it is advised that you use a scanner or spectrum analyzer to scan the whole radio spectrum. With the help of these gadgets, which provide you up-to-date details on signal behavior, you can spot any problems.

## Fixing Issues during Testing

❖ **Fake Positives:** You can come across fake positives during the testing process, which are situations when legitimate signals are wrongly thought to be forbidden frequencies. To lessen the impact of this effect, make sure your programming's settings are correct. Making sure the broadcast frequencies and tone squelch are set correctly must be part of this. To get rid of the false results, change these parameters as needed.

- ❖ **Interference:** This phenomenon occasionally appears as interference on a blocked frequency. There are a few possible causes of this interference, including nearby frequencies. You could want to install more filters to lessen the quantity of crosstalk or change the radio's antenna sensitivity to fix this problem.
- ❖ **Software updates:** Out-of-date firmware can occasionally result in strange behavior when frequency blocking is being employed. Check the software on your Baofeng radio to make sure it's the most recent version. Manufacturers often offer updates to fix problems and enhance the equipment's functionality.
- ❖ **Read the documentation:** If you're still having trouble using your Baofeng radio, you should review the paperwork that comes with it and the CHIRP program. Manufacturers regularly provide repair tools and Frequently Asked Questions (FAQs), which can help you figure out how to fix technological issues.

# Establishing and Maintaining a Novel Configuration

Establishing and Keeping Up a New Configuration: Protecting Your Exchange In radio communication, developing and sustaining a new radio configuration is similar to developing a plan for safe and effective information sharing. It takes accuracy and painstaking attention to detail to ensure that your channels, frequencies, and settings are all perfectly matched to your needs. This section will serve as the starting point for a journey through the creation and storing of your own arrangements. As we go along, we'll talk about how important it is to keep a journal of the setup of your radio.

## How to Maintain the Most Up-to-Date Scheduled Configuration

- ❖ It's time to connect your radio. First, use a programming cable that is suitable for your Baofeng radio and attach it to your computer. As you start the programming procedure, make sure your radio is turned on and operational.
- ❖ Configure the CHIRP: Open the CHIRP software on your desktop. You can easily adjust and modify the settings thanks to a connection known as CHIRP that exists between your computer and your radio.
- ❖ To download from the radio, navigate to the "Radio" menu in CHIRP and choose the "Download from Radio" option. This will download the most recent configuration from your radio and show all of the stations, frequencies, and settings on your computer screen.

❖ Modify the configuration: Make any required changes to the setup, such as adding or deleting frequencies, changing the quiet settings, or correctly adjusting the broadcast power levels. You may make sure that your radio is exactly adjusted to fit the needs of your discussion by following this step.

❖ To save your configuration after you've finished modifying it to your liking, simply select "Save As" from the "File" menu. It is advisable to name your configuration file something that is easy to recall and describes the specific situation or reason it was created.

**For several reasons, it's a good idea to keep an eye on the settings:**

❖ **Instant Restoration:** Having a stored configuration file allows you to quickly restore your radio to its original state in the event that you unintentionally change any of the settings or lose any data. Reduced downtime is experienced, and communication is always maintained.

❖ **Scenario-Based Profiles:** You can make scenarios-specific profiles by maintaining track of different stored configurations. Having these profiles easily accessible makes switching between radio networks and meeting various contract criteria considerably easier.

❖ **Documentation and compliance:** Whether for business or legal purposes, keeping track of your installations has proven to be a useful way to establish that you are abiding by the law and operating standards. It proves that the rules have been followed, which might be quite important in particular sectors of the economy.

❖ **Effective and Consistent:** Stored configurations help to improve processes' effectiveness and consistency, which in turn improves efficiency and consistency. They save you from having to manually change your radio's settings every time you use it, letting you focus on talking instead of configuring it.

❖ **Accidental Damage:** In the unfortunate event that something goes wrong, a stored configuration can act as a buffer against unintentional damage. It guarantees that your radio is ready to respond quickly in emergency situations—situations where time is of the essence.

❖ **Easy Sharing:** Sharing stored settings can help to simplify the process of making sure that everyone is in agreement while working in a team or group. It improves consistency and harmonizes communication patterns between individuals.

# Enhancing Your Baofeng Radio Show with Added Instructions and Criteria

You are studying Baofeng radio skills and CHIRP programming, but there are other concepts and practices that might help you communicate more effectively over the radio. These insights can speed up the process while also guaranteeing that your frequency block selections stay robust and consistent.

## Ideas to Improve the Performance of Baofeng Radios

- ❖ **Antenna Matters:** The antenna on your radio is what connects it to the outside world. Purchasing high-quality antennas made for the specified frequency bands could be a wise decision. An outstanding antenna can significantly enhance both sending and receiving.
- ❖ **Battery Management:** Managing batteries well is essential, especially while working long hours or traveling. Purchase a high-capacity battery pack or always have extra batteries on hand to avoid unplanned power interruptions.
- ❖ **Regular firmware updates:** Baofeng will improve the software on your gadget. Most of these updates consist of new features that can further increase the radio's usefulness, performance improvements, and bug fixes.
- ❖ **Channel Organization:** To guarantee appropriate channel organization, clearly label your channels and explain their purposes. This makes switching frequencies easier, especially when things are moving quickly.
- ❖ **Take into account investing in a second speaker-microphone.** This can streamline operations and enhance audio quality, especially in noisy settings. You may also talk on the phone and protect your radio at the same time.

## Preserving Frequency Block Setups

- ❖ **Regular Audits:** Verify your frequency block's settings once in a while. Make sure they still meet the legal and marketing standards for your business. Given that laws and frequency allocations are prone to change, this is quite important.
- ❖ **Records:** Carefully list every frequency you've chosen to block. Provide the reason for the block, the date it will happen, and any relevant legal references. For maintenance and security purposes, this paperwork may be essential.
- ❖ **Examine and evaluate:** Make sure the frequencies you've prohibited are regularly blocked. By being proactive, you may shield your radio from unsolicited broadcasts.

- ❖ **Update whenever necessary:** If your contact changes or if interference starts to appear on previously unblocked frequencies, be ready to modify your block settings.
- ❖ **Backup configurations:** You should make backups of your frequency block settings, just like you would with radio installations. In the event that you unintentionally make changes or lose data, this offers a backup.

By following these extra guidelines and best practices, you can get the most out of your Baofeng radio while protecting your frequency block settings. Remember that running a radio requires both skill and responsibility. In this constantly changing sector, you need to be well-read and ready for anything. Regardless of your experience level or length of time as a radio enthusiast, these techniques can assist you in confidently and precisely navigating the airwaves.

## Setup for the Baofeng UV-82

In order to configure your Baofeng UV-82 on a Mac, you need two items:
- ❖ A programming wire made by Baofeng
- ❖ Software for chirp programming

Chirp is an open-source program for ham radio programming. Its free version is available to all hams or anyone who needs to program a Baofeng radio. You will need it to configure your Baofeng UV-82, so please get it from the Chirp website. Double-clicking Chirp will allow you to use it without having to install it. Chirp is not signed, thus your Mac OS may decide to stop using it. If this happens to you, all you have to do is enable it in the system settings.

**Setting up your Baofeng UV-82 on a Mac is really simple. Here's what has to be done:**

> - *Read the radio's configuration*
> - *Modify or add your parameters*
> - *Write the modified configuration to the radio*

If everything goes as planned, you will be able to set up your radio. Let's analyze it.

## How to use a Mac to program the Baofeng UV-82 and read the radio

❖ It's a good idea to study the setup instructions before programming a radio. Most writing tools for radio don't even let you write to them without first reading them.

❖ To differentiate Chirp from the others, we must read the radio before we can make any adjustments to it. You can find the radio's mode by following the instructions below

❖ Go to Radio > Download from Radio after launching Chirp.

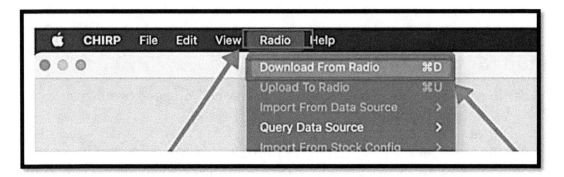

❖ Choose UV-82 as the radio model and Baofeng as the vendor after selecting the serial device that has the setting wire attached to it.

❖ Click OK to see the radio's configuration.

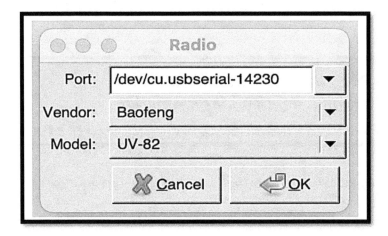

❖ Simply follow the on-screen instructions before selecting "OK."

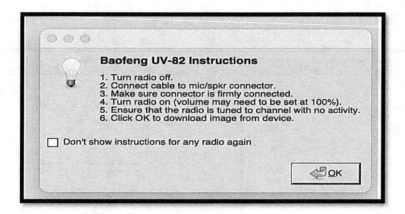

❖ If everything proceeds as planned, this window will open.

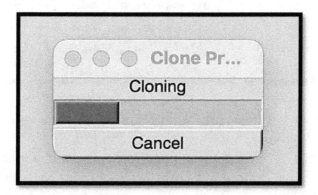

❖ Select Memories from there to add as many channels as you require.

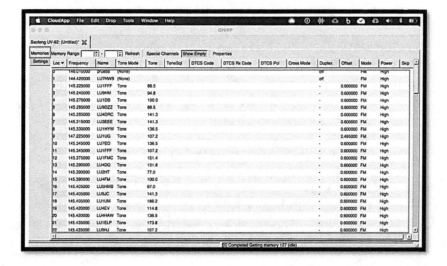

❖ Next, adjust the radio's settings to your preferences.

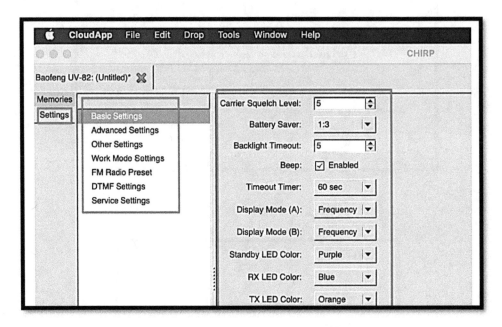

❖ When everything is finished, the radio needs to receive the settings. Choose Radio from the menu, and then click Upload to Radio.
❖ Same in terms of model, manufacturer, and kind. Choose "OK" to move forward, and then adhere to its instructions before clicking "OK." Wait for the copying to be finished. That's all there is to it. CHIRP may now be used to configure your Baofeng UV-82 from a Mac OS.

**Reminder:** The steps and processes remain the same for Windows.

By customizing your Baofeng radios using CHIRP software, you can get the most out of them and communicate efficiently in a variety of situations. Whether the user is an emergency responder, a radio enthusiast, or someone who simply enjoys listening to radios while outside, Baofeng radios can be enhanced in functionality and customization choices by adding CHIRP.

## Transferring one radio program to another

"Radio cloning," a fantastic function of the Baofeng UV-82 lets you copy settings from one device to another with ease. This feature makes it easy to swap between radios, ensuring that they are all configured consistently. When a Reference (Master) radio and a Copy (Slave) radio are connected via a particular link, data is copied between the two devices.

This is a comprehensive guide on radio cloning:

- ❖ **Connect Adapters:** Fasten the copying cable adapters to the Reference and Copy radios' auxiliary cable connectors.
- ❖ **Turn on Copy Radio:** Turn on the radio that is supposed to receive the copied settings, the Copy radio.
- ❖ **To activate Copy Mode**, first switch on the Reference radio by pressing and holding the [MONI] button. By doing this, the Reference radio enters copy mode, transferring its settings to the Copy radio.
- ❖ Copying can begin as soon as the Reference radio is in copy mode and the screen reads "COPYING," which means that data can be sent. Data transfer will be shown by the Reference radio's LED flashing red if the connection is successful. The Copy radio's LED will blink green in tandem, indicating that data is being received.
- ❖ **Copying procedure Completed:** The copying procedure is finished when both radios' LEDs stop flashing. The settings that were copied over to the Copy radio will be implemented when the radios automatically restart. Both radios should now be setup with the same parameters if the process was successful.

## Concerning Automated Number Identification (ANI)

In dispatch settings, radios can rapidly identify themselves to the dispatcher because of a crucial tactic. When using this method, which is also known as PTT-ID or Automatic Number Identification (AIN), radios must transmit a data burst including their ID code at the beginning or end of a transmission. Furthermore, ANI is activated by the Baofeng UV-82 using the DTMF signal.

**The following steps must be taken in order to configure the ANI/PTT-ID Code:**

- ❖ To use the Baofeng PC application, connect the radio to a computer and turn it on.
- ❖ To open the DTMF Encode/Decode box, select DTMF from the Edit menu.
- ❖ To open the Read from Radio window, select Read from Radio from the Program menu.
- ❖ Press the "Read" button. The radio's status LED will glow red when data is being transferred.
- ❖ Find the ANI Code box and fill it up with the relevant ANI code information.
    - ✓ In the DTMF Encode/Decode box, you can enter up to 15 group ID numbers from the list on the left. The station information box allows you to send them to each station separately.
- ❖ If you would like to send the ID before a normal message, choose the checkbox next to "Press PTT to Send".

- ❖ If you select the "Release PTT to Send" option, a standard message will be sent before to the ID being broadcast.
- ❖ From the Program menu, choose Write to Radio once again. This will cause the Write Data to Radio window to open.
- ❖ Press the "Write" button. While data is being received, the radio's status LED will glow green.

If the radio and PC are still linked, can you take the next actions to fully activate the ANI settings?

## How to use the ANI Settings: Set Up, Turn Off, and Turn On

- ❖ Open the box for optional features. To access the Optional Features box, navigate to the "Edit" menu and choose "Optional Features".
- ❖ **Read from Radio:** To start reading the current radio settings, select "Read from Radio" from the "Program" option.
- ❖ Click the "Read" button to start the reading process. When data is being sent from the radio to the PC, the status LED on the radio will flash red.
- ❖ **Set up PTT-ID:** Find the PTT-ID drop-down list in the Optional Features box. This gives you the option to decide whether the ANI data burst should happen at the BOTH (beginning of transmission) or end of transmission (eOT). To fully deactivate ANI, select "OFF" from the drop-down menu if preferred.
- ❖ **Write to Radio:** To enter the Write Data to Radio window, go back to the "Program" menu and choose "Write to Radio".
- ❖ Click the "Write" button to start the writing process. When the radio's status LED becomes green, it means that the PC is sending data to it.

If these instructions are followed, the Baofeng radio will be correctly configured for ANI operations in line with the selected PTT-ID settings.

## Channel Naming and Saving

- ❖ Use the up and down button keys to access the Memory option.
- ❖ Press the radio's Menu button. Next, hit the Menu key.

❖ Using the arrow keys, choose the memory channel you want to store, and then press the Menu button.

❖ Click the Menu button after choosing the preferred channel frequency.

❖ The Menu and arrow keys can be used to reach the Name field.
❖ Press the Menu button after entering the channel's desired name on the keyboard.
❖ Use the Exit button to save the channel.

Baofeng UV-5R two-line radios can only show the Name, Frequency, or Number of one memory spot at a time. **This is true for both of the two memory slots. To overcome this limitation:**

❖ Adjust the A and B settings separately.
❖ Configure the name to appear on channel A and the frequency to appear on channel B.

❖ Configure the receiver to simply listen to the channel that is being watched in order to avoid any potential issues.

❖ While in channel mode, use your pre-programmed station (such station 12) concurrently on A and B. In this case, A will show the nickname associated with your channel name, and B will provide the frequency. With this workaround, you can see both the channel name and the frequency at the same time, giving you the information you need even with the little display.

## The Power-On design Note

The power-on message on your Baofeng radio cannot be changed unless you use the Baofeng PC application. Assuming that the Baofeng software is already loaded **and operational and that your Baofeng radio is linked to your PC, you can accomplish this by following these steps:**

❖ Verify that your computer and Baofeng radio are connected before launching the Baofeng PC software.

❖ Select the "Other" option from the menu bar of the program. As a result, the text box with the label "Other" will show up.

❖ The "Power on Message" part of the chat box has two text boxes that show lines that will show up on the radio's LCD screen. Enter the terms you want to use in these fields.

❖ After typing the text, select "Write" from the program's menu. The changes you make to the radio are activated and preserved by this step.

❖ Verify that the Baofeng radio's menu option 38 is set to "MSG".

It is important to realize that the LCD screen on the Baofeng UV-82 radio can only show seven characters on each line. Check to see if the text you typed is inside this range.

## DIY Exercises

1. What are the process involved in Analyzing and Determining Block Frequencies?
2. Explain The Blocked Frequencies arrangement
3. Discuss the Setup procedure for the Baofeng UV-82
4. Explain How to use a Mac to program the Baofeng UV-82 and read the radio
5. What do you understand by the Automated Number Identification?
6. Explain the Set Up, Turn Off, and Turn On in ANI Settings
7. Carry out the Channel Naming and Saving

# CHAPTER TEN
# CONCERNING COMPREHENSIVE ADVANCED RADIO COMMUNICATION

## Two Bands' Applications

A radio with dual-band capabilities can send and receive signals across two different frequency bands. Very High Frequency (VHF) and Ultra High Frequency (UHF) bands are commonly included in Baofeng radio designs. People can communicate on different frequencies within these two bands since these radios can flip between them. UHF frequencies are located in the 400–520 megahertz (MHz) range, while VHF frequencies are found in the 136–174 MHz range. There are benefits and drawbacks to every frequency band. In an open area, VHF transmissions are more effective and have a longer range than UHF emissions, passing through both buildings and vegetation. This suggests that VHF can be used outside or in less crowded places.

However, UHF signals work better in cities and other places with plenty of barriers because they can travel through buildings and other structures more easily. UHF transmissions also function better indoors and in crowded spaces. Users of dual-band Baofeng radios can easily switch between VHF and UHF frequencies when the situation demands it. This makes it possible to communicate over a range of terrain and at both longer and shorter ranges. Due to this, these radios are useful in many situations, including playing outdoor sports, using amateur radios, also known as ham radios, and making emergency connections. In summary, dual band Baofeng radios are capable of transmitting and receiving data on both VHF and UHF frequencies. Customers can choose the frequency band that best fits their needs using this feature, regardless of whether they're in an urban, rural, or mixed environment.

## Examining Two Bands' Potential

❖ **Frequency variety:** Compared to single-band radios, Baofeng dual-band radios can handle a broader variety of frequencies. Typically, they can function on VHF frequencies of 136–174 MHz and UHF frequencies of 400–520 MHz.

❖ **Communication Options:** Users have a variety of communication options available to them when they are able to switch between VHF and UHF bands.

Although UHF has a greater ability to transmit past obstructions than VHF, it is more appropriate for long-distance communication in cities and other areas with lots of impediments.

❖ **Flexibility:** Dual-band radios from Baofeng can be used in specific situations. You can use the VHF band, for example, if you need to communicate over a wide region of land in an emergency. In densely populated areas or other places where signal transmission blockages may arise, the UHF band might function better.

❖ **Use of Amateur Radio (Ham Radio):** People interested in amateur radio (Ham Radio) usually prefer dual-band radios because of their capacity to receive multiple frequencies. This can be very helpful for sending digital signals, music, or data, as well as for enabling communication inside specific ham radio bands.

❖ **Channels and Programming:** A large number of VHF and UHF frequencies can be stored and accessed by users using the programmable channels found on most Baofeng radios. This feature makes it easier to switch between frequencies that are used by different organizations or for different reasons.

❖ **Interoperability:** A few dual-band radios have the capacity to receive on one channel and send a signal gain on the other. This is known as cross-band repeat. This can help establish contact over greater distances or enable communication across a variety of radio frequencies.

❖ **Enhanced features:** Dual-band radios can have extra features like dual-watch or dual-receiving, which let users send and receive messages on two different frequencies at the same time.

❖ **Learning Curve:** For those who are just starting out, the dual-band capabilities may initially seem intimidating due to the multitude of settings and options. Nonetheless, users can make efficient use of these features for communication if they allow them some time to become used to them.

## Making Use of the Cross-Band Repeat Function

### Transmitter with a Compact Cross-Band

The project's goal is to set up two transceivers from the Baofeng/Pofung series to be used as a distant base, a transmitter for Fox Hunt, and a mobile cross-band one-way repeater. All the links and criteria needed to set up these features are included in this thorough setup guide.

The following are required for this setup:

> - A pair of Baofeng/Pofung series transceivers
> - A 2.5mm/3.5mm audio cable

## Regarding the connection

Put the audio wire's 2.5 mm end into the first Baofeng transceiver's top jack. This device will be the receiver. The 3.5 mm end of the same audio line must be attached to the bottom jack of the second Baofeng transceiver. It is this group that will do its broadcasting.

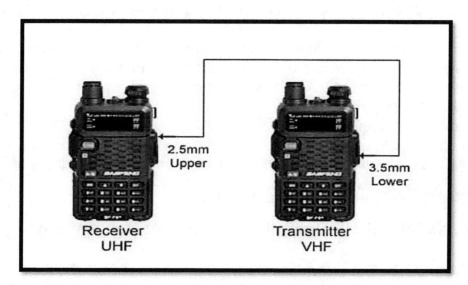

- ❖ **VOX Activation: The** voice-operated exchange (VOX) on the transmitting (TX) unit needs to be turned on. You can change the VOX Level to suit your tastes:
  - ✓ **VOX Level 1: The** transmitter (TX) switches off about two seconds after the receiver (RX) ceases to be silent.
  - ✓ At VOX Level 10, the TX level drops instantly, followed by the RX delay closing.

Turn up the volume on the receiving radio (RX) until you're comfortable.

# Field Activities: Extra Tips

## Conserving Power

- ❖ To save electricity, turn off unnecessary features like the ABR display lights and Roger Beep.
- ❖ For better outcomes, use high-end antennas like J-Poles.
- ❖ To minimize crosstalk, place the RX antenna at least 15 feet above the TX antenna.

# Separation and Isolation

## Choice of Frequencies

Change one radio's frequency to UHF and the other to VHF to minimize interference.

- ❖ To avoid signal interference, choose frequencies that are as widely apart as you possibly can. Avoid multiples of frequencies to avoid harmonics.
- ❖ Using a sound at 147.0 MHz as an example, problems may arise at 441.0 MHz from its third harmonic.
- ❖ Separation of Antennas
  - ✓ Increase the spacing between antennas to lessen radio interference.
  - ✓ There is less interference when there is more space between the antennas.

# Duplexers for Single-Antenna Use

## Cross-band VHF/UHF Operation Using Just One Antenna

- ✓ Because VHF and UHF waves do not interfere with one another, both radios can use the same antenna in conjunction with a dual-band duplexer. This enables cross-band transmission with a small dual-band duplexer such as the MFJ 916B or Opek DU-500.

## Employing the Same Band for Operation

- ✓ A single-band duplexer is necessary for both radios that share the same band of operation.
- ✓ These, however, are frequently more expensive, so they might not be the best option for this simple work.

## Employing Duplexers

- ✓ Duplexers may not work as intended outside because they are made to be used both indoors and outdoors, especially in the rain.
- ✓ Avoid using duplexers outside in the rain or snow to prolong their lifespan and maintain optimal performance.

Baofeng radios function better, are less disruptive, and are more helpful when certain settings and considerations are used for a variety of applications, such as cross-band activities and field power conservation.

# Modes of Digital and Encryption

## Comprehending Digital Modes (such as DMR and D-Star)

Using digital modes techniques such as DMR (Digital Mobile Radio), D-Star, and others, information can be transmitted over radio waves. Each method for data encoding and decoding has its own set of rules and procedures to make radio channel communication clear and effective. Baofeng radios are preferred by amateur radio enthusiasts because of their cost and adaptability. Depending on the type and software, these radios can have a wide range of modes, including digital and analog.

**A brief summary of some common digital modes is provided below:**

- ❖ "Digital Mobile Radio," or DMR for short, is a commonly used abbreviation in corporate and recreational radio. Time-division multiplexing, well known for its efficient bandwidth management, allows two conversations to take place on the same channel. Talk groups are a common tool used by DMR radios to facilitate talks.
- ❖ D-Star (Digital Smart Technologies for Amateur Radio) is another digital talk and data technology used in amateur radio. It was created by the Japan Amateur Radio League (JARL). Among its features are digital chat, data, and even GPS data that is sent in real time.
- ❖ Yaesu created System Fusion, a piece of software (C4FM). This type of digital communication blends digital and traditional speech. Among other things, it has the ability to record and transfer audio.

It is important to make sure that the Baofeng radio you want to use and the digital mode you want to use are compatible. For digital mode to work, you might also need to connect new devices or upgrade the program.

Use these procedures to set up digital modes on a Baofeng radio:

❖ **Check Compatibility:** Make sure the Baofeng radio you wish to use is compatible with the digital mode (DMR, D-Star, etc.) that you want to use. Check to see if the Baofeng type supports digital modes before attempting to use it.

❖ **Programming:** Set up the radio's frequencies, talk groups (if DMR is being used), and any other required settings in accordance with the selected digital mode. To configure your radio, you might need compatible software and connections.

❖ **Firmware Updates:** Some radios' firmware can be updated to enable digital mode or provide new features. Check to see if the firmware for your Baofeng model has been updated to enable digital mode.

❖ **Use the Correct Accessories:** If you're using a digital booster or hotspot, you might need to use one that is compatible with the mode you're using.

Recall that using digital modes typically necessitates a deep comprehension of the setups and techniques unique to each mode. Additionally, especially when utilizing amateur radio, it is imperative to abide by the regulations and secure the necessary authorizations for radio contact.

## Putting Encryption into Practice for Secure Communication

It can be difficult to use radios for encrypted private communication due to technology limits and some governmental prohibitions, especially when using amateur radio or public bands. Several countries have limited or completely forbidden encryption on particular radio frequencies in an effort to preserve clear and understandable communication. Private communication, however, might be appropriate in some permitted bands or for specific uses, including public safety or governance.

Think about the following if you want to use encryption for radio communication:

❖ **Rules and Legalities:** Before utilizing encryption, make sure you are complying with all applicable local radio rules and laws. Some places forbid private communication on certain frequencies or without the necessary permissions. Find out what the rules are in your area and for the frequencies you want to use.

❖ **Authorized Bands/Modes:** Encryption may be used by certain approved radio services or modes. For example, within the permitted spectrum of certain government, commercial, or public safety radio services, there are ways to safely communicate. You might be able to use encryption if you have permission to use these bands.

❖ **Specialized Systems:** Some corporate systems, like DMR, P25, or TETRA, can safeguard data. However, in order to use these systems, you frequently need specialized equipment and licenses, which might be difficult to get or prohibited when utilizing public radio or amateur radio.

❖ **Open-Source Encryption:** In certain situations, open-source encryption methods may be used provided they don't break any laws. They might not offer the best level of security, but they might give you some privacy. Some applications, including WAVE and FreeDV, offer a certain degree of security for digital voice transmissions across ham radio bands.

❖ **Privacy Measures:** You can use codes, selective calls, or lesser-known modes to raise the amount of secrecy in your conversation without actually hiding anything. Achieving total encryption might not be possible.

❖ **Respecting Security and Privacy:** Make sure that no encryption or privacy setting you may be using is interfering with any essential services, such emergency contacts. Put the security and safety of the public service ahead of any personal relationships.

# Combining GPS and APRS

GPS and APRS (Automatic Packet Reporting System) functions cannot be added to a Baofeng radio without the radio's suitable tools and the know-how to configure it for APRS transmission. You'll need to utilize different devices and connections to connect to Baofeng radios because the majority of them don't include GPS or APRS.

The following basic lesson describes how to pair GPS and APRS capability with a Baofeng radio:

❖ **GPS Unit:** You'll need a separate GPS device to find your location. These GPS units often come with cables that connect to the radio, and in order for them to work with your Baofeng model, they may need specific setups. Check that it is APRS compliant and transmits the required information output.

❖ **(APRS TNC):** An APRS TNC is required to connect the Baofeng radio to the GPS and APRS system. It is responsible for encoding and decoding APRS packets between the radio and the GPS. It is advised that you choose a TNC type that works with the GPS unit and your Baofeng radio.

❖ **Connections & Wiring:** As directed, connect the GPS unit and APRS TNC to your Baofeng radio. Usually, to do this, the right connections are used to link the GPS unit to the TNC and the TNC to the Baofeng radio.

❖ Verify that the APRS TNC and your Baofeng radio are set up to be able to communicate with one another. The right frequency, baud rate, and other settings need to be established in order for the GPS, TNC, and radio to be able to communicate with one another.
❖ **Testing:** After everything has been linked and setup, use your Baofeng radio to test the settings to ensure that the GPS data is being broadcast over APRS. Make sure your broadcasts follow the rules and APRS frequencies that are assigned to your area.

## Turning on and Using GPS Functions

When this feature is used, a wealth of data can be retrieved, such as your exact longitude and position, elevation above sea level, date and time, and much more. It can also show your speed when you drive or walk if you're in motion.

**To turn on the GPS gadget manually:**

❖ To access the main menu, press the (Menu) button.
❖ Scroll down and select GPS.
❖ Choose whether the GPS is on or off.
❖ Select GPS On to turn on the GPS device.

Alternatively, you can use the Customer Programming Software (CPS) to achieve this. Go to Public → Optional Settings → GPS/Ranging after opening the app. On the resulting page, enable GPS and select Get GPS Positioning. Your radio's GPS sensor will stay turned on by default when you reprogram it.

**It is easy to manually retrieve the GPS data once the device is turned on:**

❖ To view the main menu, use the (Menu) button.
❖ To access the GPS, swipe downward.
❖ If you select GPS Info, the radio's LCD screen will show all of the GPS data.

Additionally, one of the unique keys can be programmed to display this information fast by pressing a button. For instance, I have the PF3 key configured to momentarily display GPS data when pressing. To manually complete this, utilize the CPS interface or the settings.

# The Automatic Packet Reporting System (APRS) is introduced

The Automatic Packet Reporting System (APRS) is a digital amateur radio communications system that is primarily used to track individual positions, send and receive tactical information in real-time, and transmit other types of data. It was founded by Bob Bruninga, WB4APR, in the early 1980s. Since then, this versatile method has been the norm for amateur radio operators everywhere. Using amateur radio frequencies, the APRS system enables users to transmit and receive small data packets over the air. These packets contain a wide range of data, including SMS messages, weather reports, GPS position data, tracking information from far-off devices, and more.

A few crucial components of APRS are as follows:

- ❖ **Position Reporting:** One of APRS's most important capabilities is its ongoing tracking of stations' locations. Users can share their altitude, latitude, and longitude information using GPS technology. This enables other users to view their whereabouts on digital maps nearly instantly.
- ❖ **Instant messaging:** Administrators can SMS one another from station to station via APRS. This functionality can be used for information sharing or for worker-to-worker contact during events or scenarios.
- ❖ **Weather reporting:** Weather stations that have the necessary gear are able to provide weather information via APRS. Air pressure, temperature, humidity, wind direction, and speed are among the variables covered by this. It offers a particular weather report that is visible to other users.
- ❖ **Object tracking:** Users can create, follow, and keep an eye on sites using APRS. Maps display objects because they can symbolize a wide range of concepts, such as machinery, cars, and significant sites.
- ❖ **Telemetry and Sensor Data:** Through APRS, remote sensors can transmit any kind of recorded data, including voltage, current, temperature, and more. Either automatically or at predefined intervals, this data can be sent.

AX.25 is commonly employed for encrypting data sent across amateur radio channels, while APRS uses many frequencies for operation. By sending and receiving signals via a network of digipeaters, also known as "digital repeaters," it expands the reach of communication. This technology has been used in weather reporting, emergency communications, search and rescue operations, automobile tracking, public service announcements, and other innovative applications within the amateur radio community. APRS has always developed, adding new features and enhancing its functionality. It can now be used as a useful and adaptable tool by amateur radio operators who perform a variety of tasks.

## DIY Exercises

1. Discuss the Two Bands' Applications
2. Explain some of the Two Bands' Potential
3. Explain some common digital modes
4. Mention some steps in turning on the GPS gadget manually
5. Explain Automatic Packet Reporting System and its crucial components

# CHAPTER ELEVEN
# LICENSING AND COMPLIANCE WITH REGULATIONS

## About FCC Registration and License Requirements

Radio frequency usage and talk phone laws are governed by the Federal Communications Commission (FCC) in the United States. This holds true for Baofeng radios as well.

The following crucial information regarding Baofeng radio licenses and FCC registration should be known to you:

- ✓ **FCC Part 95 Regulations:** Part 95 of the FCC's regulations applies to Baofeng radios, especially the small transceivers. Furthermore covered by Part 95 are Personal Radio Services (PRS), such as General Mobile Radio Service (GMRS), Family Radio Service (FRS), and Citizens Band Radio Service (CBRS).
- ✓ **License-Free Activities:** In frequency bands set aside for license-free operations, Baofeng radios can be operated without an FCC license. For instance, FRS radios can only use particular frequencies and have a 0.5 watt maximum power limit. They can be used by anybody without a license.
- ✓ **GMRS Licensing:** Baofeng radios on GMRS frequencies allow for stronger broadcasts and longer contact ranges, but each radio user—including family members—must hold an FCC GMRS license. GMRS licenses are good for 10 years and let you use GMRS frequencies as long as you follow the rules.
- ✓ **License Application:** Individuals must submit an application through the FCC's Universal Licensing System (ULS) and pay the required fees in order to obtain an FCC GMRS license. You will need to submit your application along with your selected call sign, identity, and contact information.
- ✓ **Following the rules:** When using Baofeng radios, it's important to follow FCC rules about power limits, emission standards, antenna requirements, and frequency usage. If you make changes without permission, use frequencies that are forbidden, or produce excessive power, you may break the law and face fines.
- ✓ **Educational Resources:** The FCC website offers standards, educational materials, and Frequently Asked Questions (FAQs) to help radio users understand how to operate, obtain a license, and comply with FCC laws.

Learn how to utilize these tools so that you can use Baofeng radios legally and ethically.

✓ **Amateur Radio (Ham) Operations:** Among those who use particular amateur radio bands for communication, amateur radio operators (Hams) are also big fans of Baofeng radios. An FCC amateur radio license (Technician, General, or Extra class) and passing an exam are required in order to use a Baofeng radio on amateur radio bands.

✓ **Compliance Checks:** The FCC carries out enforcement actions and compliance checks to make sure that radio users, like Baofeng radio operators, follow the law, technical standards, and license requirements. Fines, license suspension, and other legal penalties are possible outcomes of breaking the regulations.

# How to File an FCC License Application

Fill out FCC Forms 159 and 605, which include your application for a commercial operator license, and send it back to the FCC along with proof that you passed the required written and/or telegraphy exam(s). This task can be completed electronically thanks to ULS. Public Notice DA 15-72 has caused the FCC to stop approving licenses. On your application, you must provide your email address. As soon as your application is approved, you will receive an email with a link to print your official copy of your card.

## License holders have access to ULS and can download legal permissions

✓ Enter your login, password, and FRN, or your FRN and password, to gain access to ULS Online Filing.
✓ Choose Apply for a New License from the menu on the left side of the screen.
✓ Using the drop-down menu, pick Radio Service for the recently obtained license.
✓ To continue with the application, click "Continue."
✓ Once your application has been signed, click "Submit Application."

Remember to sign your name on the application by filling in the relevant spaces with your first and last names. A Proof of Passing Certificate is not required when applying for a Restricted Radiotelephone Operator Permit (RR). Most Commercial Operator License Examination Managers (COLEMs) prepare these exams for the people who take them. See if this is a service that your COLEM provides to its customers. If you would want to submit the required documentation directly to the

FCC, please see the instructions below. You must submit FCC Form 605 in ULS in order to maintain the validity of your license. REMEMBER THIS ESSENTIALLY: For the duration of their lives, everyone who obtained a commercial radio operator license on or after May 20, 2013, will not need to renew it. Check the Terms of Licenses to determine whether you need to make any changes if you got your license prior to that date.

## Maintaining and operating while the application is being processed

Before the FCC acts on the application, the applicant has ninety days from the date of filing to exercise the rights and privileges of the sought operator license. The applicant's license to operate commercial radio equipment cannot be revoked, suspended, or the subject of a pending suspension procedure.

## License requirements

For the duration of the holder's life, permits are granted for the following:

- ✓ Permit for Restricted Radiotelephone Operator
- ✓ Limited Use Permit for Radiotelephone Operators
- ✓ Permit for Marine Radio Operators
- ✓ License for General Radiotelephone Operator
- ✓ The license for GMDSS radio operators
- ✓ Limited Radio Operator's License for GMDSS
- ✓ License for GMDSS Radio Maintainers
- ✓ Radio Operator/Maintainer License for GMDSS
- ✓ Licence for Radiotelegraph Operator

The subsequent licenses have a five-year expiration date:

- ✓ Certificate of Third Class Radiotelegraph Operator
- ✓ Certificate of Second Class Radiotelegraph Operator
- ✓ First Class Certificate of Radiotelegraph Operator

These licenses may be renewed for a maximum of five years following their current expiration date, or for ninety (90) days prior to that date. It is not required to take the test once more. The required written and/or telegraphy exam(s) must be retaken by applicants once the five-year suspension period expires. If your license has expired, you are not allowed to operate a radio.

# The pilots licensed as radio operators by the FCC

The FCC requires that a Commercial Radio Operator License be held in order to operate airplane radios. Pilots may find the term "commercial" puzzling, but remember that the FCC, not the FAA, defines it. Many pilots are exempt from the requirement for this code because of the significant exception. You don't need the license if all you do is use a standard VHF radio and you never travel overseas. The FCC Commercial Radio Operator License is available at different levels. Pilots can operate radios with a less important license called a "Restricted Radiotelephone Operator Permit (RR)". The majority of recreational boat radiotelephone stations, airplanes, and aviation ground stations are covered by this permit. A few radio devices that are frequently seen in airplanes are transponders, radio altimeters, radars, and guiding radios.

To use them, you do not require an operator license. Survival radios do not require a license, similar to ELTs. There is no exam required for the Restricted Radiotelephone Operator Permit. You must be a citizen of the United States or have permission to work there in order to be eligible. In addition to being aware of the laws, treaties, and regulations that radio stations are required to abide by, you also need to be able to speak, hear, and write. For the purposes of this discussion, let's say that you are unable to work legally in the United States but that you still require a license in order to use the equipment that comes with an active FCC radio station license. You may then be eligible to obtain a Restricted Radiotelephone Operator Permit with Limited Use, or RL. All you need to do to obtain the license is visit the appropriate sections of the FCC website, complete the required paperwork, and pay the required amounts.

# Form FCC 605 is required for admission

## Understanding the FCC Rules

All Americans who utilize or are employed in the telecommunications sector are subject to the Federal Communications Commission's (FCC) rules. The Federal Communications Commission (FCC), a separate entity of the US government, is in charge of regulating communications by radio, television, wire, satellite, and cable both within and between states. Their main goal is to guarantee the accessibility, effectiveness, and user-friendliness of these communication services. It additionally aims to foster innovation and competitiveness in the industry. The FCC essentially oversees the assignment of radio frequency bands. There is a restricted spectrum of frequencies that can be used for radio transmission, including television broadcasts, Wi-Fi, and cell phone signals. The Federal Communications Commission is in charge of overseeing the bandwidth allocation procedure in order to maximize its use and avoid conflicts between different services.

Ensuring adherence to net neutrality standards is among the most crucial parts of FCC regulations. Internet service providers (ISPs) shouldn't favor or discriminate against particular websites, applications, or services when it comes to internet traffic. We call this net neutrality. The FCC has rules in place to protect net neutrality, but because of court challenges and changes in leadership, these policies have changed. The FCC oversees numerous other facets of the internet sector in addition to net neutrality and frequency sharing. In addition to licensing regulations for phone companies, cable operators, and stations, the business also contains laws regulating acquisitions and mergers to prevent monopolistic activities. Furthermore, the FCC works to ensure that everyone has access to information services, especially in underdeveloped or rural areas. This entails ensuring that phone services are accessible to those with disabilities and that a greater number of people have access to high-speed internet.

## Comprehending Local Laws

✓ **Tower Siting and Zoning:** The Federal Communications Commission (FCC) sets regulations for the locations of communication towers and antennas in order to maximize bandwidth use and minimize disturbance. However, zoning laws enforced by local governments set limits on the locations, heights, and aesthetics of these constructions. In order to build transmission equipment, people and businesses need to follow FCC rules as well as municipal land laws.

- ✓ **Broadcasting and Cable TV:** At the federal level, the FCC is in charge of licensing and programming rules for cable TV companies and broadcasters. However, contract terms, public access channels, and station sites may be impacted by local laws. Requirements for local content and community access may be included in local governments' franchise rights agreements with cable operators.
- ✓ **Wireless Facility Deployment:** To promote 5G and the expansion of the internet, the FCC has put regulations in place to make it easier to build wireless infrastructure like small cells and antennas. However, this procedure may be affected by local regulations that outline what permits are needed, how things should look, and where they can be erected. Communities may also pass laws regulating how telecommunications companies use public rights-of-way.
- ✓ **Emergency communications and public safety:** Emergency signals, 911 services, and systems that help first responders communicate with each other are examples of public safety communications that are handled by both local and federal governments. The effective operation of disaster response and communication networks necessitates cooperation between federal, state, and local institutions.
- ✓ **Cable Franchise Renewals:** FCC rules governing the conditions and terms of franchise renewals must be followed by cable companies. Franchise agreements are normally negotiated and approved at the local level, taking into account factors such as franchise pricing, local programming requirements, and service quality criteria.
- ✓ **Consumer Complaints and Enforcement:** The Federal Communications Commission (FCC) is responsible for managing consumer complaints and enforcement actions pertaining to national telecommunications services and regulations. However, complaints within their respective domains could alternatively be handled by local consumer protection groups. This may entail paying bills on time, receiving good service, and following advertising laws.

## Following the guidelines that apply to regional frequencies

Businesses and individuals operating within a certain geographic area that use communication equipment that depends on radio frequencies must be aware of and adhere to local frequency laws. These rules are designed to be used in conjunction with Federal Communications Commission (FCC) legislation to guarantee proper radio frequency management and shield users from interference. When using radio transmitters or other communication equipment that uses certain frequency bands, it is imperative that you secure the required permits or authorizations in order to abide by local frequency restrictions. This is an important step in the compliance procedure. Usually, the local regulatory agencies or groups in charge of monitoring the spectrum utilization in the region grant these permits. Municipal frequency regulations may also contain clauses that permit other parties operating within the same jurisdiction to coordinate their usage of the frequency. Ensuring efficient spectrum usage and reducing interference are the main objectives of this coordination, particularly in high-density locations or scenarios where several users share restricted frequency bands. Worse yet, local regulations can require that radio frequency equipment adhere to particular certification standards and restrictions. This ensures that other users sharing the same frequencies won't be disturbed or interfered with by the device.

## Requirements for getting a license outside of the United States

Outside of the US, different countries may have quite different licensing requirements for Baofeng radios. This is true because radio equipment use is governed by laws that are unique to each nation. Any individual or organization that wants to use Baofeng radios legally in other nations needs to be fully aware of these rules. The Federal Communications Commission (FCC), a prominent participant in radio communications regulation, is in charge of monitoring radio communications in the US, including the use of Baofeng radios. Different license or permit requirements apply depending on the purpose, such as amateur radio operations, General Mobile Radio Service (GMRS), or Family Radio Service (FRS). Permission requirements also differ. For example, using Baofeng radios inside amateur radio frequency bands requires a technician, general or extra class license from the Federal Communications Commission (FCC). In a similar vein, Industry Canada, a government agency, oversees radio equipment in Canada, including Baofeng radios. Any individual or group planning to use Baofeng radios is required to follow Canadian legislation. Depending on the services and frequency bands being used, obtaining authorizations or certificates could be required.

For instance, in order to use Baofeng radios for amateur radio operations, radio operators in Canada must hold an Amateur Radio Operator Certificate from Industry Canada. The Radio Equipment Directive (RED) is the legislative framework that controls the use of radio equipment, including Baofeng radios, inside the European Union (EU). This rule lays out the requirements for safety, electromagnetic compatibility (EMC), and radio frequency compatibility. Additionally, the usage of

Baofeng radios may be subject to additional license or permit requirements in each EU member state. This is especially true for amateur radio, commercial radio services, and personal use.

The UK requires that radio equipment adhere to the applicable standards established by the UK Telecommunications (EMC) Regulations and the Office of Communications (Ofcom). Amateur radio operators must obtain a current amateur radio license from Ofcom in order to utilize Baofeng radios for professional amateur radio operations in the United Kingdom. Similarly, the Australian Communications and Media Authority (ACMA) control the usage of radio equipment, including Baofeng radios. Australia has several license requirements based on the type of business, services to be offered, and frequency bands to be used. For instance, in Australia, a certificate of proficiency from the Australian Communications and Media Authority (ACMA) is needed in order to use Baofeng radios for amateur radio operations.

## Limitations on Radio Frequency (RF) Exposure

The Radio Frequency (RF) Dual Exposure Limits are a set of regulations designed to shield individuals from electromagnetic fields when they are near radios, particularly those manufactured by Baofeng radios. These limitations were implemented in order to shield individuals from potential health hazards associated with prolonged exposure to radiofrequency (RF) radiation. Most nations have government agencies that draft and implement laws pertaining to radiofrequency radiation. These groups include the Federal Communications Commission (FCC) in the United States, the International Commission on Non-Ionizing Radiation Protection (ICNIRP), and other similar organizations across the globe. Radios and other devices that emit radio frequency radiation are subject to laws. When using the radio in accordance with official standards, there are some criteria that must be followed to guarantee that its electromagnetic energy stays within allowed limits.

The RF exposure limits consider variables like:

- ❖ **Specific Absorption Rate (SAR):** This method calculates the body's rate of absorption of radiofrequency energy in response to disturbances in electromagnetic fields. One common unit of measurement for radiation that aids in defining the safe threshold is watts per kilogram (W/kg).
- ❖ **Frequency range:** A large range of frequencies can be absorbed and transferred by the body at varying depths and speeds. Different radiation levels for different frequency bands are usually specified by legislation.

139

❖ **Power Levels:** The quantity of radiofrequency radiation emitted by a radio emitter is dependent on its power output. At lower power levels, there is often less contact between the components.

Baofeng radios are subject to the same RF exposure limitations set by the national authorities as other commercial transceivers. It is recommended that users adhere to the safety measures specified by the manufacturer while broadcasting. Maintaining a specific distance between the body and the radio antenna is one of the instructions. Despite concerns about potential deleterious health effects of radiofrequency (RF) exposure, it is crucial to keep in mind that scientific study has not yet yielded conclusive evidence that emissions of radio frequencies that are within allowable limits are damaging to human health. Nevertheless, in order to prevent unnecessary engagement, it is advisable to adhere to the given safety guidelines. To guarantee compliance and safety, it's essential to adhere to the manufacturer's guidelines for antenna installation and operation. When transmitting, especially, stay away from the radio receiver. Make sure you abide by the laws and regulations that regulate the maximum amount of radiofrequency radiation to which you can be exposed in your locality.

## DIY Exercises

1. Explain some crucial information regarding Baofeng radio licenses and FCC registration
2. Explain how to File an FCC License Application
3. What are the License Requirements?
4. What do you understand by the FCC RULES?
5. What do you understand by Local Laws?
6. What are the Requirements for getting a license outside of the United States?
7. Explain the Limitations on Radio Frequency (RF) Exposure

# CHAPTER TWELVE

# THE PERFORMANCE OF INSPECTIONS AND MAINTENANCE

## Two-Phase Radio Cleaning and Sanitization

Baofeng radios require regular cleaning and sterilization to maintain their functionality and guarantee user safety, particularly in crowded or shared areas.

Here's how to disinfect and clean Baofeng radios correctly:

❖ **Compile Cleaning Materials:** Prior to beginning, assemble the cleaning supplies you'll need, such as:

- Microfiber cloth or soft lint-free cloth
- Mild soap or disinfectant solution (preferably alcohol-based)
- Cotton swabs or small brushes
- Isopropyl alcohol (70% concentration or higher)

❖ **Turn off the radio:** To prevent any electrical dangers or damage, make sure the Baofeng radio is turned off before cleaning.

❖ **Eliminate External Debris:** Gently wipe the radio's exterior of any dust, dirt, or debris using a dry microfiber cloth. Keep an eye out for any ports, buttons, or nooks where dirt may collect.

❖ **Clean with Soap Solution:** Gently clean the radio's outer surfaces with a microfiber cloth dampened with a light soap solution or an alcohol-based disinfectant spray. If you want to stop fluids from getting inside the gadget, don't soak the towel.

❖ **Sanitize Buttons and Controls:** To clean the radio's buttons, knobs, and controls, use cotton swabs or tiny brushes that have been lightly moistened with isopropyl alcohol. Make sure the alcohol doesn't seep into the internal components of the radio.

❖ **Thoroughly Dry:** Before turning the radio back on, makes sure it is totally dry by wiping off any remaining moisture with a dry microfiber towel after cleaning.

- ❖ **Cleaning and disinfecting Headsets and Microphones:** To stop the spread of disease and germs, clean and disinfect headsets and microphones separately using the same procedure if the Baofeng radio has them.
- ❖ **Routine Maintenance:** Include routine cleaning and maintenance for Baofeng radios in your schedule, particularly if they are shared by several people or used regularly. This guarantees optimal performance and helps extend their lifespan.
- ❖ **Steer Clear of strong Chemicals:** Baofeng radios should not be cleaned with strong chemicals, abrasive cleaners, or excessive moisture as these materials can harm the device's internal parts and impair its functionality.

# Extending a two-way radio's battery life

- ❖ **Selecting the Right Battery:** Use high-quality, compatible batteries with your Baofeng radio. Select batteries with higher capacity ratings if you want to increase the amount of time between charges.
- ❖ **Battery conditioning:** Fully charge and repeatedly drain a battery several times before using it for the first time. This helps to optimize the battery's performance and capacity over time.
- ❖ **Maximizing Transmission Power:** Use the setup with the lowest transmission power possible to enable effective communication. Higher power levels tend to drain the battery more quickly, therefore it's best to adjust the transmit power based on the distance and communication needs.
- ❖ **Modifying Squelch Settings:** Change the squelch level as necessary to minimize power consumption from unnecessary noise and interference. Increased squelch settings can help conserve battery life by reducing the radio's sensitivity to weak signals.
- ❖ **Monitoring Battery Voltage:** To ensure that the battery voltage is being checked on a regular basis, use either an external voltage meter or the radio's built-in battery indicator. Recharge the battery before it becomes dangerously low to prevent over-discharge, which might shorten its lifespan.
- ❖ **Temperature Control:** Avoid placing Baofeng radios in extremely hot or cold temperatures as they can both shorten battery life. Use and store the radios within the recommended temperature range to extend battery life.
- ❖ **Utilizing Battery Saver Modes:** Baofeng radios have battery saver modes that automatically reduce power consumption when the device is not in use. Use these modes during times when there is less communication traffic to conserve battery life.

- ❖ **Using Energy-Efficient Accessories:** Use low-power earpieces or headsets as energy-efficient accessories to prevent further battery depletion. Steer clear of unnecessary attachments that shorten the radio's battery life.
- ❖ **Having Extra Batteries:** Keep extra batteries or portable battery packs on hand in order to keep communication going during extended activities. Rotate batteries frequently to distribute consumption evenly and prevent depending too heavily on older, less efficient batteries.
- ❖ Regular maintenance is necessary to extend the battery life of Baofeng radios. Keep them clean and well-maintained. Cleaning the battery connections and charging ports on a regular basis will ensure proper communication and efficient charging.
- ❖ **Power Management Features:** Learn about the automated power-off periods and low battery voltage alarms that are part of the Baofeng radios' power management features. Make these adjustments to effectively save battery power while satisfying your operating needs.

## Appropriate Methods for Storing Batteries

- ❖ **Charge before Storage:** Prior to storing Baofeng radio batteries, make sure they are fully charged. A fully charged battery maintains its optimal performance and helps prevent depletion when being stored.
- ❖ It is recommended to always use the original chargers that Baofeng supplied, or equivalent chargers suggested by the manufacturer. Avoid using third-party chargers as they are unable to meet safety or compatibility standards.
- ❖ **Avoid Overcharging:** Avoid leaving Baofeng radio batteries on chargers for an extended period of time after they are fully charged. Overcharging not only reduces battery life but also raises other safety concerns and can lead to overheating.
- ❖ **Store in a cold, dry place:** Choose a cold, dry location to store Baofeng radio batteries. When utilizing batteries, it is best to stay out of extreme temperatures, direct sunlight, and high humidity as these conditions can reduce the batteries' lifespan and performance.
- ❖ **Optimal Temperature Range:** Store Baofeng radio batteries in the temperature range recommended by the manufacturer. Batteries can sustain damage or have their capacity reduced due to extreme heat or cold's effect on their chemistry.
- ❖ **Avoid Complete Discharge:** While it's important to use Baofeng radio batteries on a regular basis, avoid letting them run entirely empty before storing them. To maintain a battery's health, it is preferable to just partially drain it.

- ❖ **Inspect for Damage: Prior** to storage, check batteries for signs of corrosion, leakage, or damage. Damaged batteries should not be stored since they may not function correctly and may even be dangerous.
- ❖ **Employ Battery Cases:** Consider using protective covers or battery cases to store Baofeng radio batteries in an appropriate manner. These accessories help lower the chance of physical harm and exposure to the environment.
- ❖ **Rotate Stored Batteries:** Be sure to rotate several Baofeng radio batteries when storing them. You can ensure that each battery is utilized evenly and maintains its capacity by doing this.
- ❖ **Regular Inspections:** Make that stored batteries are generally in good condition and have the proper amount of charge. If a battery's charge drops below a predetermined point, replenish it to prevent a deep discharge.

## Guidelines for Continuous Maintenance

- ❖ **Inspection and Cleaning:** The radio's exterior should be cleaned on a regular basis with a soft cloth and a light cleaning solution. Keep an eye out for any signs of damage, loose parts, or corrosion. If required, wipe contacts and connections using a cotton swab that has been lightly moistened with isopropyl alcohol.
- ❖ **Battery Maintenance:** Comply with the safe battery charging and storage instructions previously provided. Check the battery's capacity and condition on a regular basis. Replace a battery if it starts to lose power or show signs of degradation.
- ❖ **Firmware Updates:** Stay informed about firmware updates from Baofeng. Keep an eye out for firmware updates on your radio and, if necessary, update the firmware by following the directions. Firmware changes often feature bug fixes and performance improvements.
- ❖ **Upkeep of Antennas:** Regularly inspect the antenna for deterioration or wear. Make sure the antenna and connection contacts are clean for optimal signal transmission. Replace any worn-out or damaged antennas.
- ❖ **Programming and Settings:** Verify and update the radio's programming and settings as needed. Verify that the channels, frequencies, and settings are configured to meet your needs. Make regular backups of your programming data in case the radio needs to be reset or updated firmware.
- ❖ **Protection of the Environment:** Keep Baofeng radios away from extreme heat, moisture, dust, and collisions. Use covers or protective cases if the radios are being transported or stored in a harsh environment.
- ❖ **Function Testing:** Perform routine function testing to ensure that the radio's features and functions are working as intended. Examine the broadcast and

receive capabilities, channel scanning, squelch settings, and emergency functions (if applicable).

❖ **User Training:** Constantly provide users with instruction on proper radio usage, protocol, and emergency procedures. Verify that users understand how to operate the radio effectively and safely.

❖ **Documentation and Records:** Maintain a log of all radio maintenance activities, firmware updates, programming adjustments, and issues that occur. Preserve documentation of battery inspections and replacements for future use.

❖ **Expert Assistance:** Seek professional guidance from accredited Baofeng service centers or specialists in the event of technical difficulties or repairs beyond standard maintenance. Avoid making unauthorized repairs or changes that could void the warranty or compromise security.

## DIY Exercises

1. Discuss how to disinfect and clean Baofeng radios correctly
2. What are the steps of extending a two-way radio's battery life?
3. What are the Appropriate Methods for Storing Batteries?
4. What are the Guidelines for Continuous Maintenance?

# CHAPTER THIRTEEN

# SOPHISTICATED RADIO PERFORMANCE

## The Radio Range: How Far Can It Go?

Which other avenues of communication could they be able to use? What is the distance in kilometers? Most people think about this before spending a lot of money on a brand-new two-way radio. It's essentially the most often asked question. But if you go through the comments on that same station, you can find that other disgruntled people are also moaning about how short it is. Some say it's only fifty yards, some say it's three, five, and so on. Why are they so different? Mostly because the terrain and the equipment may have a substantial influence on the talking range. Two-way radio advertisements usually claim a reach of "up to 36 miles" or more. This commercial uses the wording "up to" as keywords. This upper bound is more theoretically based than it is empirically supported. How far in advance are you going to speak? The main factors influencing antenna range are obstacles, antenna type, signal power (wattage), and signal type. It's possible that no one component increases the number of people who hear your message. When combined, though, they might make the difference between a device with a half-mile range and one with a six-mile range or more. Let's talk about each one separately.

## Various Types of Indication

To begin with, not all radio wave transmitters are made equally. They have different gaits and responses to what they come across. Frequencies less than 2 megahertz (MHz) can therefore follow the curvature of the Earth since they are reflected off of the atmosphere. Therefore, radios positioned below the horizon may occasionally pick up these low-frequency broadcasts, even at hundreds of kilometers away. Generally speaking, anything can travel farther at a lower frequency. Since many of these features are located in the HF (High Frequency) band, which spans from 29 to 54 MHz, CB radios and certain HAM frequencies can access them. Conversely, low frequencies are more likely to result in several additional problems.

## What is superior, UHF or VHF?

These days, the most common frequency ranges used by two-way radios are Very High Frequency (VHF) and Ultra High Frequency (UHF), commonly known as "frequency bands". We frequently get asked, "Is UHF or VHF better?" None is superior to the others on their own because they all have advantages and disadvantages. Compared to UHF frequencies, VHF frequencies have the ability to pass through objects more readily. Additionally, VHF will go farther. When two waves are sent across a clean zone, the VHF wave travels through it roughly twice as quickly as the UHF wave. You yell, "Sign me up for VHF!" Wait a minute. While VHF is more effective in sending signals over obstacles and farther, it is not always the best choice. This is because UHF and VHF frequencies respond to structures differently, in case you're wondering "Why?" It's crucial to keep in mind that when you're inside or near a building, UHF transmissions are shorter than VHF signals. To help us grasp this better, let's look at an example. Assume for the purposes of this illustration that you are attempting to contact a person across a corporate building. There is a three-foot gap in the midst of a metal wall. A metal object is radio wave resistant.

The VHF wavelength is approximately five feet wide, while the UHF wavelength is approximately 1.5 feet huge. The door is barely 1.5 feet long; therefore the UHF signal may easily travel through it. The VHF signal gets reflected through the door, though, because it is wider than the door. It is evident that UHF navigates packed spaces in buildings more effectively to reach its goal. Internal building metal is likely to cause interference to VHF transmissions. Thus, it's basically a compromise. However, if you intend to use the radio outside where you will have a clear line of sight, the VHF frequency is a preferable choice because of its stronger signal. The standard heuristic is this one. However, if you wish to use your radio in towns, highly forested areas, or in or near buildings, you should consider using UHF instead of VHF. This is because UHF transmissions can more easily flow through structures than VHF signals because they are less likely to be blocked. The ability to avoid certain "dead spots" in and around buildings (UHF) (Virtual High Frequency) is exchanged for increased range.

## The antennas

Examining your antenna more closely is one of the simplest ways to increase the range of your device. We neglected to mention your antenna when we said, "The maximum communication range is the distance to the horizon." When computing distances, your antenna's height is taken into consideration. Put another way, the height of the antenna affects the exact distance to the horizon. The distance to the horizon dependent on height can be calculated using a formula, albeit a complicated one. For now, let's just adhere to one essential principle: When a transmission antenna is placed six feet apart at both the transmit and receive ends of the transmission, its maximum range is about six miles. Therefore, a portable two-way radio with a five watt power output may have a maximum dual range of six miles for two individuals who are around six feet tall. This is done in an unobstructed, level, and open space. Will it ensure that the six miles are reached? No. You might get four kilometers, or maybe not even that much. How can you get it to get closer to six miles than it does to four miles? Make advantage of an antenna with greater power!

## Concerning the obstacles

Remember how we said you might be limited to four miles? Every now and then, big things can block radio transmissions. It is not advisable for radio communications personnel to work with metal. Under normal conditions, it won't be able to transmit radio waves. Ever wonder why microwaves and glass doors don't work well together? Have you ever noticed that there are tiny gaps in the metal mesh that covers glass doors? Little signal waves are emitted by microwaves at very high frequencies. Microwaves are far bigger than the pinholes in the metal mesh, despite their tiny size. The microwaves are prevented from venting from the oven by the metal mesh. The steep terrain is another thing to take into account. Radio signals cannot travel over hills, unlike those made of metal. If you reside in an area that is hilly, you should be aware of this. However, a wide variety of non-metallic items, including people, furniture, stone, drywall, and several other materials, have the ability to transmit radio waves. Conversely, a radio signal loses strength when it travels through an object. Moreover, a larger reduction in signal strength is observed with increasing item density. This implies that a signal's range decreases with the number of things it goes through.

## Increasing the Range of the Transmission

❖ **Choose the Correct Frequency:** Baofeng radios frequently function on a variety of frequency bands, such as UHF (Ultra High Frequency) and VHF (Very High Frequency). Selecting the right frequency for these radios is crucial. Identifying the frequency band that is currently in use is the first step towards selecting the appropriate frequency. It is crucial to consider your communication needs as well as the terrain you will be working in when selecting the right frequency band. In comparison to the UHF frequency range, the VHF frequency range is typically greater in outside and public areas, whereas the UHF frequency range is preferable in inside and urban contexts.

❖ **Using a High-Gain Antenna:** To extend the radio's broadcast range, it is suggested that the standard antenna be swapped out for a high-gain construction. The application of high-gain antennas can increase the achievable coverage as well as the signal strength, particularly in larger open areas. Make sure the antenna fits both the model of your Baofeng radio and the frequency range it operates in before making the purchase.

- ❖ **Antenna Positioning Optimization:** To achieve the best possible performance, the antenna should be positioned vertically. Through optimization, this configuration improves both signal transmission and reception. Steer clear of any impediments or metallic objects that might hinder or interfere with the transmission of the radio signal. There is also the option of increasing the transmission range by using elevated areas, like tall buildings or terrain. You can achieve this by using elevated scenarios.

- ❖ **Changing the Power Output:** Baofeng radios allow you to manually change the power send quantity. It is recommended that you utilize greater power levels when you are communicating over longer distances or in areas that are challenging to navigate and contain obstacles. It is important to strike a balance between concerns about the level of power output and the duration of the battery's life, bearing in mind that higher power levels demand more battery power.

- ❖ **A Clear Line of Sight:** It's critical to confirm that the stations transmitting and receiving signals have a clear line of sight. By doing this, the communication range will be increased and the degree of signal attenuation reduced. Placement of the radio equipment and yourself should be such that there are as few obstacles as possible, such as large buildings, thick foliage, or topographical features that could potentially block radio signals. You will be able to get the best response possible as a result of this.

- ❖ **Using Repeaters:** If you have access to repeaters, you should utilize them to extend your Baofeng radio's transmission range. A piece of hardware known as repeater equipment has the ability to receive signals on one frequency and retransmit them on another. This is the reason they are able to effectively cover a wider area with their coverage. To utilize the repeater efficiently, you must coordinate with the local operators of the repeater and obtain the relevant permits or access codes.

- ❖ **Optimizing Radio Settings:** You should adjust the parameters to get the best possible performance from your Baofeng radio if you want to maximize its potential. Assuring that the radio is set to the proper frequency, modulation mode (such as FM or NFM), and squelch level will help to minimize background noise and enhance signal clarity. You must familiarize yourself with the features and workings of the radio in order to take full advantage of the chances it offers.

❖ **Routine Maintenance:** Regular maintenance on your Baofeng radio is crucial. This include checking that the battery is functioning properly, cleaning the contacts, and looking for any signs of damage to the antenna. To preserve the highest degree of reliability and performance, it is essential to replace worn-out parts or accessories as needed.

# Reception-focused antenna positioning

❖ **Vertical Orientation:** In most cases, the antenna must be oriented vertically in order to receive the maximum possible amount of reception. This site can increase the signal's power because it is in line with the polarization of most radio frequencies.

❖ **An Unobstructed Line of Sight:** The antenna must be positioned so that it faces directly towards the source or the station transmitting the signal in order to guarantee a clear line of sight. It is crucial to stay away from structures, trees, and metal objects that can impede or weaken the signal.

❖ **Elevated Position:** Whenever it is feasible, place the antenna at a high spot. When it is possible to do so, this should be done. As a result, the available line-of-sight vision will be maximized, and the amount of signal attenuation caused by ground-based impediments will be minimized.

❖ **Outside Placement:** It is imperative to place the radio and antenna outdoors in an open space devoid of any large buildings or topographical factors that could potentially obstruct reception. The process ends with this phase, which is the fourth.

❖ Locations outdoors receive greater reception than those inside, generally speaking.

❖ **Preventing Interference:** Since interference can be caused by the antenna, it is imperative to keep it away from any electromagnetic interference sources. Power lines, electrical appliances, and electronic devices are some of these sources; they can all have an adverse effect on reception quality and noise levels.

❖ **Directional Antennas:** A directional antenna, like a Yagi or log-periodic antenna, should be pointed towards the transmitting station or signal source that you want to receive. We refer to this as a directional antenna. Consequently, the signal intensity will increase and the reception will become more focused.

❖ **Angle Adjustment:** You should research your options for modifying the antenna's tilt or angle if you wish to optimize the reception. The quality and strength of the signal can vary significantly even with little alterations to the antenna's orientation. This is the kind of event that occasionally occurs.

- ❖ **Antenna Height:** Broadly speaking, a higher antenna height improves reception by reducing the amount of ground reflections and improving line-of-sight clarity. This is as a result of less ground-ground reflections. When it is practical, the antenna ought to be placed atop a tower or at a higher elevation.
- ❖ **Appropriate Grounding:** Make sure the antenna is grounded correctly to prevent static buildup, reduce interference, and improve the receiving system's overall performance.
- ❖ **Consistent maintenance.** Regular maintenance for the antenna necessitates cleaning, inspecting it for corrosion or damage, and properly connecting it to the radio equipment. One may help ensure that the reception's quality stays at the highest possible level over time by doing routine maintenance.

## Techniques for Increasing Signal

**Make effective use of the gain antenna to increase the radio signal.**

Should both radios make use of the identical gain antenna, their respective transmission and reception efficiencies will both increase. Could you tell me how the gain antenna works? What methods does the satellite use to identify communication indicators? According to one theory, the frequency will increase in a way that is proportionate to the satellite's distance from the real Earth. Given the ionosphere and the considerable distance between the locations, it is expected that the loss will rise. For what reasons are satellite communication signals able to use a transmission frequency higher than 5GHz? More precisely, this is because the gain antenna can provide loss-free signal reception while compensating for the loss of available space. Additionally, adding a gain antenna to the radio might enhance the amount of available space that is sent by decreasing the amount of space that is lost.

The methods exist for resolving the interference:

- ❖ Elevate the radio transmission sites' elevation
- ❖ Modifying the surroundings and course of radio communication
- ❖ Boost walkie-talkies' reception sensitivity
- ❖ Boost the antenna's gain.
- ❖ Boost the radio's output power.
- ❖ Incorporate a repeater

## Elevate the locations of the radio transmitters

There's a new, kind of hip comment circulating among amateur radio enthusiasts. "Height determines everything!" would be that. More than a hundred trials have shown that this is a real thing with consistently positive results. We won't go into more depth regarding the idea here due to its complexity. Customers are provided with the following product details when they choose to purchase walkie-talkies: The communication range is three meters to three hundred and fifty kilometers. This illustrates the maximum communication distance in public areas. What would happen to you if you were standing on the mountain when the platform was installed? If you're in a really high-up building, you can still talk to your friends. That's the way things really are. The function of height is currently highly advantageous.

## Select the direction and setting for the radio communication

Making decisions about these characteristics is essential since the direction and context of communication can occasionally lead to notable variations in the quality of the connection.

**It is recommended that we adhere to these standards in every circumstance:**

- ❖ Try to choose a connecting point that is located on a higher elevation; for example, see if you can connect on the second story as opposed to the first floor.
- ❖ It is advised that communication take place outside as there is a notable attenuation and reflection of waves measuring 70 cm within the building walls.
- ❖ It is strongly advised that you try your hardest to stay away from residential areas that have buildings surrounding them. This includes areas with dense foliage, areas beneath high-rise structures, areas densely packed with buildings (like the ancient city area), sections surrounded by massive cars, tunnels and bridges, and giant metal billboards in front of you.
- ❖ As mentioned in point D, using urban canyons is a very important choice. The fact that our large cities are home to a large number of tall buildings and buildings that are closely spaced apart makes it harder to find genuine chances for communication across vast distances.
- ❖ Select an appropriate route and try to stay clear of any tall structures or metal structures that can obstruct your journey between the locations that are connected to you. This is due to the possibility that these structures will impede your advancement. Furthermore, it can function as a signal reflector if you position it behind the direction you want to connect.
- ❖ The fifth point states that connecting at night has a greater impact than connecting during the day.
- ❖ Furthermore, the connection provided by stationary points is better than the connection provided by mobile devices.

## Boost the sensitivity of walkie-talkies' reception

If both parties increase the reception sensitivity, it is the same as increasing the other party's transmission power. When modifying the radio station's reception sensitivity, it's crucial to adhere to the handbook's directions.

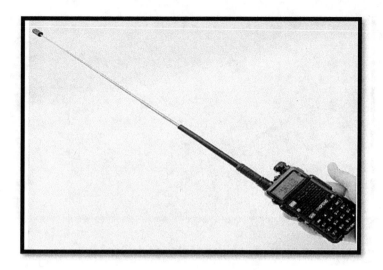

## Using transmitting antennas with high gain

Which kind of antenna would work best right now for your radio? For a certain technology, a longer antenna will frequently be longer than a shorter antenna. Regardless matter the technology, this is true. The antenna of a portable walkietalkie needs to account for the mobility of the instrument as well as the gain of the device. Certain dual-band and multi-band walkie-talkies require consideration of each frequency band when designing their antennas. As a result, your only option is to limit the amount of profit you can make. The walkie-talkie is commonly built with a helical rubber antenna, just like its original design. The gain is not very great, and the communication quality is in the middle of the spectrum despite the comparatively short antenna length.

If the prerequisites are met, users are free to buy antennas with a wavelength of ¼ or ½ on their own. The antenna offers a significant gain and passable to fairly satisfactory communication quality despite its relatively large length. Consumers that choose mobility above all else have the option of choosing a shorter antenna. The radio mobility has increased even though the gain is not that great. Using a longer antenna is one option offered to individuals that value transmission performance highly. The walkie-talkie will still be able to send and receive radio frequency signals even if it will become less portable. In addition to considerations such as length, gain, and shape, you also need to consider the compatibility of the antenna's interface with the radio's interface when choosing the antenna for the paired radio. It's critical to remember this.

## How can I maximize the antenna's potential?

On walkie-talkies, basic communication often takes place via straight-line transmission in the VHF/UHF frequency range. Transmission in this frequency band is more affected by building obstructions than by other causes. When all is said and done, it is clear that the antenna provides a height advantage. Public areas that are accessible to the general public are the best places to use two-way radios. This ensures the finest possible results. Using the antenna at its strongest point may be difficult if you are low to the ground or close to tall buildings. This is because there are situations in which it could be challenging to maximize the antenna's performance.

If the antenna is shifted horizontally over a considerable distance, the signal will probably fluctuate substantially. The UHF band is where this effect is most noticeable because of its shorter wavelength. The external antenna installed on the car will be more influential than the room intercom that just certain operators would use. The received signal strength may fluctuate if you are primarily concerned with a particular local repeater station's transmission. After that, you could want to adjust the external antenna to determine the location of the strongest received signal. This is typically the location where the most effective relay effect can happen during transmission. To determine if moving to a sizable area will help with the failing communication signal, you can try moving the location signal to the left and right. The reasoning applies now just as it did previously.

Recall that the antenna's vibrator is frequently perpendicular to its ability to transmit and receive electromagnetic waves throughout space. The antenna's ability to send and receive electromagnetic waves explains this. The walkie-talkie's antenna may broadcast and receive signals in a horizontal position while preserving directivity thanks to the use of vertical polarization, which ensures the preservation of signal quality. It is recommended to hold the walkie-talkie vertically instead than horizontally when using it. This is the result of the previously mentioned reason.

## Utilizing Radio in Plans for Emergency Preparedness

Depending on the needs of your community or group, you should first determine the most effective method of communication in an emergency. Consider things like the extent of the coverage, the type of emergency, and the manner in which you will work with organizations outside of your own. Choose the radio equipment that best meets your needs next. Considerations such as radio bands, range, durability, and interoperability with other systems are crucial. Your staff members must receive training in radio operation, communication, emergency procedures, and problem-solving techniques. Everyone must be proficient at using the radios. Provide clear communication guidelines that cover call signs, message formats, channel placements, and issue reporting procedures. These standards should be adhered to in both ordinary and emergency situations.

Working together, crisis management and local government can guarantee uniformity in interoperability protocols, techniques, and frequencies of communication. Obtain the permits and approvals required in order to use radio frequencies. Test and repair radio equipment often to guarantee that it will work in an emergency. Checking the antennas, replacing the batteries, and, if necessary, updating the software can accomplish this. This involves inspecting the gadget as well. Establishing diverse communication networks and channels would be advantageous for a number of reasons, including alerting the public to emergencies, keeping an eye on events, working with reaction teams, and sharing data. Incorporate radio communication into the Incident Command System (ICS) architecture to ensure a coordinated response to an emergency. Decision-making should be supported by radio discourse, contact checkpoints, and the assignment of radio controllers.

## DIY Exercise

1. What is superior, UHF or VHF?
2. Mention Various Types of Indication
3. What are methods exist for resolving the interference
4. Explain how to Select the direction and setting for the radio communication
5. How do you Use transmitting antennas with high gain
6. How can you maximize the antenna's potential?
7. Discuss some steps in Utilizing Radio in Plans for Emergency Preparedness

# CHAPTER FOURTEEN
# CONCERNING TROUBLESHOOTING

## Managing Typical Problems with Baofeng Radio

### There is not enough charge left in the battery

A Baofeng UV-82 battery that cannot hold its charge while being charged is one of the most common things to break. This could be due to a number of things, such as using a battery that is broken or non-functional or not charging the cell sufficiently. To identify the source of the issue, confirm that the radio's battery is fully charged and positioned correctly. If that doesn't fix the problem, you ought to think about switching to a different battery. The charger might not be as effective as it was intended to be, which would account for the issue.

### Insufficient communication or reception

Another problem that many customers encounter with the Baofeng UV-82 is inadequate transmission or reception. There are several possible causes for this, such as using the wrong frequency or having a subpar receiver. Make that the antenna is operational and correctly attached to the radio before attempting to identify the issue. Make sure the radio is tuned to the correct frequency to guarantee you receive the program or response you want to hear. If you think it's necessary, you can use the mute setting to cut down on background noise. If you are still having trouble sending or receiving the information, think about moving, or get in touch with the manufacturer for more help.

### Commands are not being entered into the keyboard

Users of the Baofeng UV-82 may find the malfunctioning keyboard to be inconvenient. This could be caused by a variety of factors, including a faulty or locked keyboard. First, confirm that the passcode lock is not engaged before attempting to see if the radio's settings have been returned to their original state. If the keyboard is still not working, it might be necessary to contact the manufacturer for more help.

### An unheard signal

Understanding what is being said may be challenging when listening to distorted audio. This problem could have a number of sources, such as an excessively loud speaker or malfunction. Verify that the speaker connections are tight and that the volume isn't set too high in order to resolve this problem. Try to see whether the distortion goes away once you turn the volume down to a level that you find comfortable. For more help, get in touch with the manufacturer if the problem persists.

## Being unable to schedule TV shows

Setting up a channel can be difficult at times, and problems do arise from time to time. Numerous factors, such as utilizing the wrong programming wire or not being in the correct programming mode, could be the cause of this. To fix the problem, make sure the radio is in the correct programming mode and that the correct programming wire is being used. If the problem persists, seek out more help by referring to the user handbook or contacting the manufacturer. It could be challenging to figure out how to change the Baofeng UV-82's menu and settings if you are unfamiliar with them. Go through the user manual and get the information required to navigate the radio's menu and change its settings in order to resolve this problem. It is crucial that you check that the radio is set to the right mode based on your preferences. For additional help, get in touch with the manufacturer if the problems persist. I hope you find that satisfactory!

The second one is not a problem in and of itself, but it could be if you don't know how to use the radio. It may be difficult to learn how to change the many settings on this specific model if you've never used one of these radios before. To sum up, the Baofeng UV-82 is a reliable and flexible radio, but like every electrical device, it occasionally has problems. If you know the most common problems and how to fix them, you may quickly get your radio working again. We recognize that it's not always easy to find the answers you need and that it's not always easy to interpret the user manual. Please try to familiarize yourself with your radio. You will understand how it works better if you use it again. If something goes wrong, you'll be able to use this to remedy the issue much faster.

## Resolving Typical Problems with Baofeng Radio Content

While configuring Baofeng radios with CHIRP is generally not too hard, there could occasionally be issues.

The list of frequent problems and their solutions is as follows:

- ❖ **Connection Errors:** Make sure the programming wire is inserted correctly and that you have chosen the right COM port in CHIRP if you have any connection errors.
- ❖ **Invalid Frequency Error:** Make sure the bands you are configuring are within your Baofeng radio's range and are legal in your area in order to avoid the Invalid Frequency Error.
- ❖ **Radio not responding:** On some Baofeng models, you have to hit certain buttons in a certain order in accordance with a specific sequence in order to get into programming mode. To determine the proper way to accomplish a task, consult the user manual or internet resources.

# Using Emergency Baofeng Radios

Baofeng radios' dependability is vital in emergency situations. As with any machinery, they might have problems and need to be maintained on a regular basis to function at their best. **This guide will assist you in troubleshooting typical issues and fixing Baofeng radios in an emergency:**

## The debugging

- ❖ **No Power:** If your Baofeng radio is not turning on, check the battery or the power source. If it stays off, carry on reading. Verify that the battery has been charged and is positioned correctly. You could try using a different battery or power source to see if there are any issues with the current one.
- ❖ **Poor Reception:** In the event that you are not receiving strong signals, it is advisable to inspect the connection between the device and the antenna. Make sure the antenna is not damaged in any way and that it is firmly attached to the radio. If you wish to improve reception, you may want to consider raising your elevation or adding an additional antenna.
- ❖ **Interference:** You should attempt changing the channel or frequency if you suffer static or interference when listening to the radio. Interference can be caused by a number of things, such as nearby electrical equipment, structures, and weather. Try out several different channels until you find the one with the least interference.
- ❖ **Audio Problems:** If you are having trouble hearing or being heard clearly, check the microphone and volume settings. Ensuring that the microphone is unobstructed and that the volume is set to a comfortable level is crucial. If

you are using an external microphone or a headset, check the connections for any evidence of damage or loose wires.

❖ **Programming issues:** If you are having trouble with the channel settings or programming, you should check the programming software and settings again. The proper channels, tones, and frequencies must be programmed into the radio. You can utilize the online resources or the user manual to get help if you need it with programming.

## Taking Care of and Maintaining

❖ **Maintain it Clean:** Use a soft, dry cloth to wipe away dust, debris, and grime from the radio's exterior on a regular basis. The radio's finish may be harmed by employing abrasive cleaners or harsh chemicals.

❖ **Prevent Moisture Damage:** Baofeng radios should be kept dry and protected from water damage by taking certain measures. When using the radio in damp or rainy conditions, put it in a protective case or cover and keep it away from excessive moisture or humidity.

❖ **Store Correctly:** Baofeng radios should be kept dry, cold, and well-ventilated when not in use. Keep them out of direct sunlight and extremely cold temperatures as these conditions can harm the components and batteries.

❖ **Examine Often:** Check the radio for indications of wear, corrosion, or damage on a regular basis. Inspect the external ports, antenna connection, and battery connectors for any problems. To stop additional harm, replace any worn-out or damaged parts right away.

❖ **Battery Care:** To guarantee optimum performance, properly charge and maintain the batteries in Baofeng radios. Battery lifespan can be shortened by not properly draining or overcharging the batteries. Observe the maintenance and replacement guidelines for batteries provided by the manufacturer.

# Explaining Protocols for Amateur Radio

Using a variety of radio frequencies, licensed radio operators can communicate with one another through the pastime and service known as amateur radio, also referred to as ham radio. While amateur radio provides many avenues for contact, operators must follow specific regulations and regulatory requirements to guarantee that their operation is morally and legally correct.

**Let's take a closer look at a few of these prerequisites:**

- ❖ **Licensing Requirements:** In most countries, including the US, operators of amateur radio equipment must get a government license in order to use it legally. Most of the time, a written test covering basic radio theory, regulations, and operating procedures must be passed in order to receive a license. It's feasible that various license classes exist, each of which gives operators a unique set of responsibilities and rights.
- ❖ **Frequency Bands:** Radio transmission via amateur radio occurs on specific frequency bands that are permitted by global regulations, such as those set by the International Telecommunication Union. Within these frequency bands, which are further divided into numerous segments, various forms of communication, including speech, data, Morse code, and amateur satellite communication, are each allotted their own segment. Operators must adhere to the usage guidelines and band plans specified by the licensing authority that granted them licenses.
- ❖ **Call Signs:** Each authorized amateur radio operator is assigned a call sign that serves as a distinctive representation of them on the airways. In call signs, a prefix indicating the operator's country or region is frequently followed by a string of characters and numbers. Usually, the operator can be identified by their call signs. During specific points in the communications process, operators must identify themselves and send using the call signs that have been assigned to them.
- ❖ **Operating Procedures:** To ensure that communication is carried out in an orderly and courteous manner, it is expected that amateur radio operators will adhere to the established operating procedures and etiquette. This entails using a call sign to identify oneself at the start and end of broadcasts, listening before broadcasting to prevent disrupting ongoing discussions, and communicating with concise and understandable language.
- ❖ **Avoiding Interference:** Radio operators need to take care not to interfere with other radio users, even if they aren't using the amateur radio bands. To do this, it might be necessary to use appropriate power levels and antenna designs in addition to following band planning and frequency usage guidelines. It might also be necessary to check for signals before transmitting.
- ❖ **Emergency Communications:** During public emergencies and natural catastrophes, amateur radio operators are crucial in supporting emergency communications. Operators are strongly encouraged to participate in training and readiness exercises even though emergency communications is subject to certain regulations and procedures. This will ensure that they are able to deliver effective help when needed.
- ❖ **Propagation and Band Conditions:** Knowledge of radio wave propagation and the conditions of the bands that amateur radio operators operate on is

essential for successful operations. Operators must to be cognizant of the factors that impact signal propagation, including atmospheric conditions, solar activity, and topography of the regions they function in, and they ought to modify their operational strategies correspondingly.

❖ **Q-Signals and Abbreviations:** Standardized Q-signals and abbreviations are widely used by amateur radio operators to convey common messages and instructions rapidly. These codes, which contain QRZ (who is calling me?), QTH (location), and QSL (confirmation), help to simplify communication and preserve bandwidth when used.

## Seven Steps to Prevent the Most Common Baofeng Radio Issues

**First off**, unlike the more expensive Japanese radios, none of the Chinese radios (many of which cost even more than the Baofeng series) can be adjusted using the keypad or free programming tools. A Baofeng radio's LCD may display the "+-" offset symbol, however this does not always mean that the radio has been set to the proper offset for the band and memory you are using. Furthermore, Baofeng handheld S-meters always show the entire scale, independent of signal strength. As a result, many consumers may believe that their signal is greater than it actually is. This applies to all Baofeng portable devices.

**Second**, if you want to buy a Baofeng and think that the FCC Part 90 approval also means that you can have two VHF or UHF frequencies on your two VFOs that are 12.5 kHz apart (or less) and not hear any cross-channel noise or interference on the other frequency, then you will need to buy a radio that is better than the Baofeng UV-5R. Many foreign sellers on Amazon or eBay choose not to ship FCC Part 90 radios because of their greater cost. This indicates that these radios cannot be used on any corporate frequency in the United States (see example below). The radio on the right passed the quality control test, in contrast to the radio on the left.

The UV-5R is a moderately cost option, but the UV-5R V2+ (introduced in late 2014), the UV-5R 8 Watt, or the BF-F9V2+ are better Baofeng receivers that can be used with many of the accessories compatible with the UV-5R series. They have better Baofeng receiver boards and aren't all that much more expensive. Look into the UV-82 range if your camera is compatible with only a portion of the UV-5R accessories. If you're ready to pay a little bit more, Wouxun and TYT both manufacture radios with better receivers, more memory (from 199 to 999), and a wide selection of accessories. A multichannel audio circuit, 10 watts of transmits power, 20 to 25 FM commercial radio channels, and audio inversion for safer communication—when available—are some of the characteristics that distinguish TYT from Baofeng.

**Thirdly**, take note that you are unable to listen to two separate discussions at the same time when using the Twin Dual Receive (TDR) option (Menu 7). You may occasionally miss a quick exchange of words or a remark on one of the two VFO receivers because the radio just alternates between them (count "1001 and 1002" to check how quickly it scans). There is currently no way to activate dual-talk on Baofeng radios; either you have to buy a higher model or utilize third-party "mods" to make it possible.

**Fourth**, if you insist on purchasing the least expensive USB programming cable, be aware that the majority of new owners are either unaware of how to properly turn off the Wind or do not read or follow the comprehensive step-by-step instructions on the various internet radio forums on how to fix issues with cheap knockoff cables. Using the radio's alpha-numeric memory naming also requires radio programming software. This is possible with many TYT radio kinds, but not with any Baofeng radio keyboard. I suggest using an actual Prolific, Silicon Labs, or FTDI 2-prong Kenwood-style programming cable to eliminate the chord problem. The majority of issues that users encounter while attempting to program their Baofeng radios can be resolved by purchasing an official cable and adhering to the guidelines posted on internet discussion boards. Alternatively, you might upgrade your radio's programming faster than you can drink your morning cup of coffee by purchasing an RT Systems cable and software package. We buy and utilize kits from RT Systems.

It may still be worth a few hours of effort for some people to try their fake $5 programming cables and freeware first, but it is still worth every penny to have people who: a) have English as their first language; b) are American ham radio operators; c) have your model radio in front of them; and d) support their product. Most data cable programming is done by three companies: Silicon Labs, FTDI, and Prolific. You never know what you'll get because the most prevalent Chinese cables are also the ones that are most frequently illegally copied. You will pay $20 to $25 for a genuine Prolific, Silicon Labs, or FTDI wire, but the money saved will prevent hours of frustration, which we have all experienced. Your buddies will quickly believe you're a Baofeng programming radio "genius" if you get the $48.95 RT Systems kit with the FTDI cable and radio software. Utilize an FTDI or Silicon Labs link if you would rather utilize free programming tools like VIP or Chirp. My preferred series of programming cords is Wouxun/Red Silicon Labs, while FTDI cables also function very well. Again, give us a call to discuss the various Baofeng software cable kits from RT Systems if you feel that your time is still valuable, or if you would just like not to bother with programming (and getting the USB cable driver to run). Even if they cost more than a phony widespread cable with free software, they are very successful at what they do. The bragging rights alone might make the $48.95 worthwhile in some regions. Because you use RT Systems' equipment, you can respond to being branded a computer "genius" in a way that's kept confidential. In addition, we provide wire kits and software for a variety of radios manufactured by other firms.

**Fifth**, older hams and engineers who believe "they" should be able to do things with it (using a different way) are the ones who moan about Chinese radios in general and this particular brand in particular the most. Their $60–$200 radio isn't working the way their $300–$600 Japanese radios like Alinco, Kenwood, Icom, or Yaesu do. They don't know why. Then, people post complaints about Chinese radios on various websites. These complaints are typically directed at unpleasant owners, radios that don't function the way "they" believe they should, or radios that lack features that they can obtain on their $300–$600 Japanese radio, such as GPS, D-

Star, and APRS. The reason friends who use Privacy Codes or PL tones on their different FRS/GMRS radios don't immediately hear them when they broadcast on the correct frequency (without a PL tone selected for transmission) is another mystery to those experiencing these issues. It's also a common misconception that only Baofeng radios are compatible with later digital trunking systems; any analog radio cannot send or receive data from any of the several Baofeng radios. If you want to monitor any local law enforcement agency that has made the switch to digital, you will need to get a digital radio or a digital scanner. Fortunately for us, some county sheriffs and the Arizona Department of Public Safety still use regular VHF or UHF radios for their operations. This frequency is readily set up to use on any dual-band Chinese radio (if you have the appropriate wire and software).

**Sixth**, be warned that you will most likely run into issues with these radios at some point if you are unfamiliar with the most recent models of VHF/UHF radios, if you do not want to follow the detailed instructions available on many Baofeng websites or user groups, or if you do not even plan to read the handbook. Most of the time, you will blame the radio while in fact, it isn't the radio's fault since, among other things, you either forgot to adjust the frequency step, which prevents the repeater audio from reaching your receiver, or you forgot to set the PL tone on both encode and decoding. I believe you ought to get a radio that has several local bands "pre-programmed" into it already. This will rely on the memory channels and features of your radio, which vary depending on the model. We can program the radio using a shared script, which will save you a great deal of time and cost you about $20 for a printing of the frequency and channel information.

**Seventh**, even though radio salespeople are everywhere, it's a good idea to look for one with a US headquarters or one who can provide you with the "straight scoop" on the various Baofeng models. It goes without saying that because they don't carry the other brand or model, dealers who only carry one brand of radio won't be able to assist you in finding one that better suits your demands. In an attempt to attract "local" business, several Chinese merchants also make the ridiculous claims that they are the only ones with direct contact to the Chinese manufacturer, that they are the only ones who can fix a specific brand of radio, and that they are headquartered in the US. It's also crucial to be aware that some merchants might take "seconds" right out of the manufacturer, which might include radios with significant flaws! We demand that we only ever receive brand-new radios—never refurbished or returned equipment. We also require that they be FCC Part 90 radios upon arrival, as many of the radios being offered online aren't intended for sale in the United States. If you are ready to take a chance on one of those merchants, there are plenty of Chinese vendors on eBay and Amazon who will gladly accept your money but want you to pay to return the damaged radio before they will refund your money. You'll be shocked at how much it costs to send your malfunctioning radio back to China. You did a fantastic job if you made it this far via reading the instructions. Keep in mind that many radios are just not calibrated correctly, and the radio's hardware is to blame for the problem. By taking these seven simple steps, you may avoid most configuration issues that new Baofeng owners encounter. You will thus be a more informed radio listener.

## DIY Exercises

1. Discuss the process of troubleshooting typical issues and fixing Baofeng radios in an emergency
2. Explain few Protocols for Amateur Radio
3. Discuss Seven Steps to Prevent the Most Common Baofeng Radio Issues

## Overall summary

To sum up, the Baofeng radio is a versatile and dependable communication tool that can be used for a range of activities, including pleasure and disaster preparedness. In this book, we have discussed many aspects of Baofeng radio characteristics and functions and maintenance techniques. The Baofeng radio's adjustable channels, long battery life, robust chassis, and intuitive interface may be useful to a range of users, including emergency responders, outdoor enthusiasts, and amateur radio operators. Baofeng radios provide an affordable and dependable means of communication in every situation, be it local, long-distance, or emergency coordination. On the other hand, optimal performance requires appropriate maintenance and care. By following the maintenance recommendations in this guide, users can prolong the life and dependability of their Baofeng radios while preserving their maximum performance and durability. In conclusion, the Baofeng radio is more than just a communication device; it may also be a savior in dire circumstances, a tool for exploration and travel, and a means of fortifying relationships between communities. Users may get the most out of their Baofeng radios and speak clearly and confidently over the airways by putting the knowledge and resources in this book to use.

# INDEX

## Y

www.ingramcontent.com/pod-product-compliance
Lightning Source LLC
LaVergne TN
LVHW081525050326
832903LV00025B/1639